"Shane has done a wonderf[...] starting and building a successful small business. His clear steps and fun stories keep the book interesting and easy to implement."

-**Ray White – author of** *Connecting Happiness and Success*

"Shane is the real deal. He is both an entrepreneur and financial guru. *Forecast Your Future* lets the reader see inside the mind of someone in the trenches of both worlds. When properly applied it will help you create a more profitable and fulfilling business venture for your future."

-**Jason Noble, Owner – Noble Installs, PlanningCenterHelp.com; Pastor, Hillside Community Church, Fort Worth Texas**

"Shane has shared his training and experience in business in clear, bite-sized, practical ways that even a Ph.D. in biblical studies can understand. Shane has helped our school see the reality of our financial situation and has provided tangible practices to guide us to our preferred future. *Forecast Your Future* is a book I will return to often."

-**Gene Wilkes, Ph.D., President, B. H. Carroll Theological Institute Author of** *Jesus on Leadership*

"It has been said, 'The best way to predict your future is to create it.' What Shane has put together is a thoughtful, practical handbook for peering into what lies ahead in your business and identifying what needs to be adjusted. Instead of the typical, reactionary principles and temporary fixes most small business leaders employ, his tested strategies help business owners get ahead of the real problems that waste resources, cause stress, and limit growth. This is a road map for making changes *now* to achieve a more successful outcome *later*. I recommend this book to anyone who is looking to create a clearer path for their business and implement a plan to see that vision fulfilled."

**-Justin Winstead, Owner,
Justin Winstead Agency, LLC**

"As an owner of multiple businesses, Shane has helped us gain clarity for making better decisions and provided insight into understanding key challenges and opportunities for growth. *Forecast Your Future* provides a framework that all businesses should adopt so they can better create value and improve opportunities for success."

-Mike Perkins, CEO, Kinsman Ventures

"This book contains a straightforward yet powerful set of principles and ideas sure to benefit anyone running a business. Through personal experience with Shane, I know he practices what he preaches with his clients on a daily basis."

**-Matt Eagleston, Executive Pastor,
Hillside Community Church, Fort Worth Texas**

"Finding Shane Bender with Bender CFO Services came at a pivotal time in our business. It had definitely grown past me and my husband and I was looking for someone to help me see past all the numbers into what I knew could be a clear prosperous future. Shane not only put together a plan and implemented it for our business, but he dug through all the mountains of chaos and developed a clear beautiful road map for us to follow. Shane and his team gave us back our peace and more time to work on other parts of our business so we could grow more! We are forever grateful for his help! We would highly recommend Bender CFO Services to anyone looking to upgrade their life and business!"

-Dwayne and Angelique Gates,
Owners - Cinemation Design

I wholeheartedly recommend this book to anyone who is in business or who advises small businesses. The clear and thoughtful insights have helped me to clarify my approach to my numerous business clients.

-Christopher Haltom, Attorney

"Shane has packed this book with practical tips and insight for business owners and leaders looking to get a handle on their financial present and future. The writing style is conversational, but the content dives right to the heart of the matter and maps out a logical path forward. Great book!"

-Kyle Gabhart, author & entrepreneur

Forecast Your Future

*How Small Businesses Exchange
Stress and Chaos for Cash
and Clarity*

SHANE BENDER

**AUTHOR
ACADEMY** elite

©2018 by Bender CFO Services Inc.

Published by Authors Academy Elite

Printed in the United States of America

Library of Congress Cataloging-in-Publication Data

Bender, Shane, 1976-

Forecast Your Future: How Small Businesses Exchange Stress and Chaos for Cash and Clarity / Shane Bender

Pages cm

Includes bibliographical references

ISBN 978-1-64085-303-4 (Hardback)

ISBN 978-1-64085-302-7 (Paperback)

1. Personal Development. 2. Business Finances
3. Entrepreneurship 4. Business Ownership

To my supporting bride, Holly, and to our kids Matthew,
Jonah, Jack, and Savannah!

Let the words of my mouth and the meditation of my
heart be acceptable in Your sight, O Lord, my rock and my
Redeemer. Psalm 19:14

CONTENTS

ILLUSTRATIONS

FOREWORD

Maybe you desire to turn your passion into a full-time gig. Maybe you just started a new business, or maybe you have been in business for a while and you need to grow. One thing is certain, cash flow and clarity matter. In *Forecast Your Future*, Shane Bender knows how to express what all business owners need to know clearly and concisely.

Who

As a business owner, the concepts in this book are essential for me and my business partner as we strive to grow our business to new successful levels. If you have goals and aspirations for your business, it is important to know what you need to do to hit those goals and assess and adjust as you go.

What

This book is not just another finance book. It is for business owners, entrepreneurs, and anyone who aspires to build a business of their own. It gives you guidelines on how to forecast your revenue, manage expenses, and control cash flow. Business profitability is important to the sustainability, growth, and impact of your business. Shane Bender gives you practical steps to help you on your journey.

When

If you don't know where you are today financially or where you are going, then you need to read and apply this now. Even if you haven't taken the time to do this in a while, invest some time working on your business and not *in* your business.

Where

Shane's book helps you:

Understand where you are today.
Determine your desired destination.
Learn how to reach your destination faster.
Learn when and how to assess and adjust along the way.

How

Shane gives you steps on building this model in a simple and flexible way. What if you wanted to make a decision and you had a model that you could tweak, and it would show you the revenue, profit, and cash flow based on key assumptions? *Forecast Your Future* shows you how by giving you the basics that all business owners need.

Why

Most of all Shane Bender helps you understand why this matters. He explains the fears and poor assumptions that business owners commonly make. Businesses thrive on revenue, profits, and cash flow. We need to be aware of issues and build consensus around our plan.

We all desire more peace and less chaos in our life. Owning a business is a challenge but it is very rewarding as we strive to combine our passion with financial security and growth.

—Kary Oberbrunner, author of *Elixir Project,*
Day Job to Dream Job, The Deeper Path,
and *Your Secret Name*

THE JOURNEY TO BUSINESS OWNERSHIP

It was late in the day at nearly 5:30. My boss (owner of the company) came into my office. It was eerily quiet and most everyone had left for the day. The Director of Human Resources was sitting in a red chair. My heart sank and fear took over. My boss quickly explained that he didn't think I was happy there and they needed to let me go. He was right about that, even though being let go scared me to death.

I had come there a year earlier with high expectations. I had come from a small business that grew revenue from $4 million to $16 million in 5 years, and it was eventually sold to a large publicly traded company. I thought that I could replicate this with the new company, but it was not the same. I was not making the impact I wanted and revenue was decreasing. There was not enough revenue for a Vice President of Finance at about $170,000 in salary and benefits, and I knew my days were numbered.

As I cleared out my office and turned in my keys, I was in a state of shock. The drive home seemed long that day, and I called my wife. She was saddened and angered by what happened. We have four kids, and at the time, they were ages three to eleven. I was the sole provider and my wife homeschools our children. The severance pay would not last long. How would I provide for my family?

A couple of days later as I sat in my closet praying and asking for wisdom, I suddenly had a thought to open the safe sitting next to me. At the bottom of the safe was an old gold watch that belonged to my father who passed away when I was only three years old. I noticed an inscription on the back that I had never read before. It said, "God Loves You, Dad." Emotions overwhelmed me as I sat there crying. I called my older brother to ask if he remembered this inscription on the watch and he did. My dad had this inscribed when he was sick with brain cancer. It was like he was speaking to me from 35 years ago. I knew that God was in control and peace came over me.

The next few months took me on a journey that I wouldn't change for anything. At the time, however, I didn't think it was great. I accepted a position as a financial advisor, following in similar footsteps of both my dad who passed away and my stepdad who raised me. I spent 10 weeks studying diligently to pass the licensing exams. For six weeks during the hot Texas summer, I walked in neighborhoods and knocked on thousands of doors to build my list of contacts. Eventually, I became a licensed financial advisor, but something was not right. I didn't enjoy much of what I was doing at all. I know there is value in being a financial advisor, but something was missing.

Since I graduated with my Masters in Business Administration from Baylor University, I had become a Certified Public Accountant and worked two years at one of the top four Accounting Firms, as an auditor. I then gained valuable experience as an Assistant Controller for four years at a $200 million publicly traded electronics distribution company. I had an entrepreneurial streak about me at the time and left this company after four years to join a very young digital marketing company that focused on paid search on Google. For the first few years, I had to explain what this was to many people because it was still so new at the time. I spent nine years there as a Controller and eventually a Director of Financial Planning & Analysis as the company grew extremely fast and it was sold to a large publicly traded marketing company. When leaving this company, I went to the small company mentioned above where I wasn't happy and I was eventually let go.

Now back to being a financial advisor. What was missing? I was not using much of my experience. I was told what to say and shown the process for growing my business as a financial advisor, and it was not exciting for me. Upon leaving this financial advising firm and interviewing for a job, I came across an organization providing fractional (part-time) CFO work. Although that organization was not the right fit for me, I realized that this idea makes a ton of sense. I had worked at two companies that would benefit from this type of service. Times had changed, and technology made it much easier to provide CFO services from anywhere. So, in January 2016, I launched Bender CFO Services, Inc.

Throughout my career, and especially since starting my CFO (Chief Financial Officer) service, I have learned much about what makes businesses successful financially. I desire to train, lead, and serve other companies and even nonprofits so they can apply these ideas and grow their companies. On top of that, I have started my own business, so I know first-hand the challenges of starting something new, focusing, and learning to grow. How can we move to the next level? With each new level, there are new devils and challenges to tackle. What do we do when we haven't been there before?

I am not going to say I have all the answers. I have consulted many advisors and there are specific situations to every company and industry. What I want to offer you through this book is a framework to build your company. It doesn't matter if you're a solopreneur, consultant, or business owner to many employees with millions in revenue. The basic framework applies.

This book is broken into four parts with short chapters and concepts. I have put some activities, downloadable worksheets and templates in the back of the book in the

Appendices. My desire is to fill this book with stories, examples, and analogies sprinkled with valuable guidance.

Part 1: Where are you financially in your business today?

The first step in a journey is to know where you are today. This concept makes sense when you are taking a trip, or you need directions to get somewhere. It is essential to know where you are before you can get to the destination.

This same concept works for a business. You should know your revenue, expenses, profit, and cash flow. Before you start getting overwhelmed we will talk about how to do this in an efficient and affordable way.

Part 2: Where is your destination?

I get how hard this can be as a business owner. We come up with ideas all the time. The revenue target changes, and we can adjust strategy quickly. We are small and nimble, but this can also be dangerous. It is best to assess a destination and focus on a goal. We will discuss how to do this while remaining flexible to changes in the industry, economy, and financial situation.

Part 3: How do you get to your destination as quickly as possible?

Most businesses want to get to their goal faster. I believe that if you aren't growing, you are dying. If you aren't learning, then you are becoming obsolete. In this section, we will discuss strategies that involve a combination of people, processes, and profits to help you get to your destination quickly.

Part 4: When and how to assess and adjust your destination?

No matter the size of a business, you must assess and adjust. I like the quote from former United States President Dwight Eisenhower who said, "In preparing for battle I found that plans were useless, but planning was indispensable." In this section, we will unpack what this means. How often should you assess your business and when to adjust? How do you know when you should adjust?

Let's get started as I desire to serve you through these pages to develop and meet the vision for your business and the freedom, peace, and enjoyment that comes with that.

PART 1

UNDERSTAND WHERE YOU ARE TODAY

Anything we do in life starts with knowing where we are currently. We start with financial mindsets such as fears and misinformation that could be driving us to chaos and stress. To some degree businesses operate a lot like people. At first, we are infants and toddlers just trying to get by and learning very quickly as we go. Eventually, we get a sustainable business, but we operate like teenagers who are not ready to grow up.

How can we develop a more abundant mindset so we can accomplish the dreams we desire? How can we overcome our fear and embrace the numbers? How do we get out of the chaos and move into more clarity and eventually more cash profits? It very much starts with taking our limiting or disempowering belief about business and finances and turning them into abundant and empowering thoughts. Once we make the switch in our head, we can start moving more quickly to the financial destination we desire.

CHAPTER 1

LESSONS FROM A SQUIRREL
AND A DRAIN CLOG

It was a cold October morning in the Rocky Mountains of Colorado. I had on two pairs of socks, multiple layers of clothes, gloves, and I carried a chair. As I walked out of sight of anyone at the bottom of the hill, I sat down in my chair for a period of reflection and prayer. Quickly, I noticed a squirrel that seemed to be upset at my presence. He sat up in a tree staring at me and making an unusually large amount of noise. Had I somehow interrupted his plans? Over the next two hours, the squirrel would run by me getting acorns and food which he buried in a hole in the ground. He was working very hard on this mid-October day.

At the end of the two hours, I was listening and taking it all in. I believe that God desires to impress wisdom upon us if we will listen. Then, I saw the squirrel run past me with food to bury for the winter. When I saw him do this, some wise thoughts came to mind. I wouldn't say it was wisdom I didn't already know, but it was a good reminder. I wrote down five thoughts about business and life in my journal from the actions of this squirrel.

1. Work Hard

The squirrel did not let me stop him from doing his work. He kept doing what he thought was important because this day was a good day to search for food. He would rest later, but not today. The food was not right there in front of him. He had to search.

It is important that we search for wisdom. Working hard also includes working smart by investing in personal development, reading, and learning. We should be consistent and do a little each day to meet our goals.

2. Focus

There was no distraction. Even though I sat there in a chair very close to the squirrel's area and probably got in the way, he kept doing what he knew was necessary and important. He focused on his goal and kept searching for and collecting food.

We should follow this example and look for ways to stay focused on our goals. There is always technology, other people, clients, and new ideas that can be very distracting. We should focus on one main goal to reach success.

3. Courage

It might have been easy for the squirrel to run and hide this day, but he chose to continue working anyway. He would run past me within 20 feet at times. He made some noise when I first got there, but did his job.

As business owners, we must continually get out and meet new prospects, network, and do things out of our comfort zone to stretch and grow.

4. Preparation

The squirrel knew through instinct that winter was coming. He was finding as much food he could and burying it in multiple holes.

It is important to work hard to expand our business when we can. We should work toward multiple products and streams of income to protect us from recessions, lost business, and a changing world. It is essential to avoid procrastination by doing a little each day to meet our goals. This might be business development, personal development, or business strategy. Yes, we should work and meet the needs of our clients. I have found that when I network, meet new people, or learn something new, it ends up benefitting my current clients in the long run.

5. Rejuvenation

There will be a time when the squirrel will relax during the winter. He will enjoy the food he was searching for today.

We all need to relax and rejuvenate to stay productive and successful. For me, just taking a trip to Colorado and spending time in reflection gave me a positive viewpoint and energy. You may think that I am stretching this analogy too far. Maybe you think this is only nature and nothing highly profound. No matter what, I felt almost enlightened after that experience. It was a great reminder, and that is why I chose to write about it.

No matter if you are thinking about starting a side business or you have been a business owner for years, these concepts are true. Through focus, working hard, courage, preparation, and rejuvenation, you can start and grow any business while weathering the storms that come.

I tell this story as you assess where you are today. We might have lost focus from the main reason we started a business. We might let others distract or discourage us. One good thing to do is to write down why you are in business. Why did you start this organization and what enjoyment do you seek from it? How are you serving and adding value to others?

The Drain Clog

Recently my bathroom sink was not draining well. I put drain cleaner down the sink and waited 15 minutes. I then ran hot water following the instructions. There was still some grossness right under the stopper that I could not reach. The sink was draining better for now. I then felt the urge to improve the situation. I didn't know how to remove the stopper, so I searched on YouTube.

I gained some confidence from watching a help video. After pulling out the stopper, I noticed a very disgusting sight that needed cleaning immediately. How had I lived so long with this right under my nose? It was making me nauseous. I felt like I needed to scour my hands under scalding hot water for 15 minutes up to my elbows. The bacteria and mold along with hair and who knows what else made this very unpleasant.

Then, I went to another sink and thoroughly cleaned the stopper. I pulled out as much of the disgusting assortment of grossness from the drain as I could. Once everything was clean, I reattached the stopper, cleaned the sink, and admired my handiwork.

The sink drained beautifully, and I found myself looking forward to brushing my teeth and using what seemed like a brand-new sink.

This experience made me see a very strong parallel to businesses. First, many of us live in the gross situation we are in. We are so used to not knowing our financials and we make gut decisions without any insight because that is what we have always done. We make decisions off the cash in the bank because that is the way it is. We constantly put out fires and work crazy hours to keep the business afloat because we are accustomed to the mess. We don't think we have time to clean it up.

Once the business gets clogged and sales are down, we are losing money, and we become overwhelmed with stress. Maybe then we might seek help. The problem is that we don't know how bad it is. Have you heard how things seem to get worse before they get better? Well, this can happen in a business also. This is scary.

When I opened the drain, it was absolutely disgusting. When you open up your business to find out where you truly are today, it might be ugly. You might not have the right employees. Your profit might be worse than you think. Your margins might be much worse than you imagined. You might have made commitments to customers at prices that likely won't make any money; at least they won't make you money with the current people and processes you have in place.

Then you attempt to figure out a way to clean up your business. This can take some time. The problem is that you still need to operate your business. You need to find the time to completely revamp and clean it up. This takes strategy, process documentation, change management, hiring the right talent, and maybe even new IT systems.

Now you are getting nervous because this is much harder than cleaning a dirty drain. We will talk about it more in Part 3 as we figure out how to get to your destination as quickly as possible.

Once everything is running more smoothly, you will look back and wonder how you ever lived the way you did. You will be more excited about your business and its growth in the future. You will be more excited about how you can service your customers.

Yes, the sink will get dirty again. You will have to review this regularly as you grow, but you won't let it get that messed up again. I certainly will keep my bathroom sink draining smoothly from now on.

Have you properly assessed your business financially? Take some time to understand your cash, revenue, expenses, and profit.

There are many reasons why we choose not to assess our business and the biggest are around mindset and fear. Next, we will tackle your financial mindset because this can make all the difference.

Call to Clarity

Take some time now to write down at least five reasons you started and want to grow your business. Keep this in a place you can visit regularly.

CHAPTER 2

FINANCIAL MINDSET MATTERS

As a finance guy, my initial thinking is to move toward the negative. I have been brought up and even trained to consider all the possibilities and to be the devil's advocate. I feel obligated to consider all risks.

The other day I was standing in line with my son to order food at a barbecue restaurant. He wanted to order something that was expensive and too much to eat. He argued with me. Then he told me to order for him. I ordered the wrong thing. He said he didn't want that. I asked him to order and he said he didn't know what to order. I was starting to go crazy. It seemed like a no-win situation.

He was in a negative and argumentative mindset, so nothing was going to work. We do this in business also. We have an idea and then someone argues all the reasons why it won't work. I must admit that I have been this person in meetings before. I remember thinking how I was merely doing my job.

In Michael Port's book *Steal the Show*, he challenges us to say "Yes, and" instead of being the devil's advocate and saying no. The devil's advocate has a way of killing off creativity and killing dialogue.

I am not saying you should not consider all the risks, but there is a time for this. Generally, this would not be good in a collaborative, creative, and strategic discussion.

The "Yes, and" approach to business is much more empowering and leads you to an abundant mindset. It exposes limiting beliefs and makes you search for a solution. You would be surprised at how many solutions are out there.

Empower Your Thoughts

When it comes to business finances, there seems to be an abundance of disempowering thoughts. I am guessing that the following statements could be part of the cause of so many business failures.

1. I don't know accounting. It's too complicated.

2. I am not good at technology.

3. I don't have the time for finances.

4. I am not a numbers person.

5. I will hire someone to do this when I can afford it.

6. I need more business and will worry about this later.

Let's go through each of the limiting and disempowering thoughts and rephrase each one into an empowering and abundant perspective.

1. **Disempowering Thought**: I don't know accounting.

   Empowering Thought: I can learn and understand the basics to help my business be more profitable.

   I believe people over-complicate accounting. I think some accountants even over-complicate it. If you are running a small business with a few products and services, it can be much easier than you think. A lack of organization and failing to keep your finances up-to-date are what make it hard. Think about what would happen if you didn't mow the lawn all summer. Your yard would be a disaster and it would be difficult to make it look nice. Even a 13-year-old can mow the lawn each week. I am not saying a 13-year-old should run your business, but you get the point.

2. **Disempowering Thought**: I am not good at technology.

   Empowering Thought: Technology can be learned, and it is getting easier. Google is my friend, and I can usually find the answer if I search.

3. **Disempowering Thought**: I don't have the time for finances.

   Empowering Thought: I have to take the time to sharpen my skills because this will increase my productivity and profitability.

   I was reading a book that was written in 1952. It claimed that people are busier and more stressed than ever and don't have time to focus and enjoy life. Apparently, this has been a problem for a while. Time and productivity are closely related. Time can be multiplied. There are tons of books written on productivity. We all make time for what is important to us.

4. **Disempowering Thought**: I am not a numbers person.

   Empowering Thought: The math is not difficult, and I have a calculator or spreadsheet to help.

   Running a business does not require complicated math. You don't need to know calculus, geometry, or even algebra. You need to know simple math such as addition, subtraction, multiplication, and maybe some division. The math does not get much harder than what you probably learned in 3rd or 4th grade. *You can be good at anything that is important to you.* We all are continually learning. There are successful people who don't have a high school diploma and still manage to do well in business. There are also people with expensive graduate educations who are in debt and close to financial disaster.

5. **Disempowering Thought**: I will hire someone to do this when I can afford it.

   Empowering Thought: I want to know enough to provide anyone I hire with direction and guidance. This will ensure that I am getting the most out of the services I am paying for.

   You have heard of hiring out what you don't want to do so you can focus on what you like to do. I don't agree with this entirely. When it comes to your business finances, you really need to understand the basics and what numbers will produce success. I am not saying that you have to do your own bookkeeping. You need to know how to take the reports you get and motivate yourself toward success. You need to ask the right questions. Keep your bookkeeper, CPA, or financial consultant honest. Have them explain what is happening and educate you on what to look for.

6. **Disempowering Thought**: I need more business and will worry about this later.

   Empowering Thought: Revenue is important, but not at the expense of everything else.

Revenue and sales are very important and the first steps of the business cycle; but other parts of the business cycle such as Billing, Collections, Payroll, Expense Management, and Customer Service are also important. Sometimes billing someone or reaching out to someone to ask if they received an invoice can spark another discussion. Business is all about contacts and touch points. We provide value in the many ways and make life easier for our clients when we communicate with them.

I want to challenge you to expand your beliefs about finances for your business. You should not outsource or delegate all financial understanding to others. As you grow, you will hire others to help you, but no matter what, you need to have the education and understanding to build financial success.

Call to Clarity

Write down at least one limiting belief you have financially, and then write an empowering thought to replace it.

CHAPTER 3

OVERCOME FEAR OF THE NUMBERS

Fear is such a common emotion and it shows up in many ways. Do you fear what the numbers are going to tell you? Maybe you don't want to see how bad the financial situation is because you don't want to make difficult decisions. Do you have any of the following fears?

- spending a lot of time to know the numbers, which results in less time with family or friends

- uncovering negative information about the numbers

- having to make hard choices and cut expenses

- having to work even harder

- worry that a spouse or friend might find out

- worry that employees could find out

- the stress of accountability

- extra anxiety and sleepless nights

- business failure and being a statistic

- getting sued

- customers could get upset and leave
- competition and the lack of revenue
- business development and rejection
- regretting going into business for yourself
- failure leading to downsizing
- missing an opportunity

There are so many fears, and I have had many of them cross my mind. In Paul Smith's book *Lead with a Story*, I came across this story with an applicable message.

Once upon a time, in a land far away, there lived a very bright and trustworthy young woman. Having learned all she could in her own village, she set out to explore the neighboring lands. After some time, she came upon a great city surrounded by a huge castle wall. "Surely, I can learn something new from the people here," she thought to herself. But after entering the city, she found its people too frightened and depressed to share any wisdom. "Why is everyone here so sad?" she asked.

One trembling citizen answered, "Today is the day the giant comes."

"Giant?" she scoffed in disbelief. "There's no such thing as giants!"

"Oh, but there is," came the response. "He stands over 10 feet tall! So tall, he can't be rightly called a man at all."

Skeptical, but intrigued, the young woman pleaded, "Tell me more of this giant."

So, the frightened citizen nervously explained to her, "Every year, on the same day, at the same hour, the giant comes down from the mountain where he lives. He stands at the edge of the clearing and yells, 'Send out your bravest man for me to fight, or I will knock down these walls and kill everyone inside!' Each year, one poor valiant soul steps out to face the giant, and there he stands, mesmerized by the giant's enormity and the impossible task ahead. And every year, the giant slays the poor warrior where he stands before he even has a chance to draw his sword. The warrior doesn't even move. It is as if he is hypnotized."

Eyes wide with fascination, the woman begged, "Can I see this giant?"

"The only way to see the giant," the citizen explained, "is to face him in battle."

Still in disbelief but eager to learn, the woman responded, "Then that is what I will do!"

At the appointed hour, the giant's distant but powerful voice was heard over the castle walls, "Send out your bravest man for me to fight, or I will knock down these walls and kill everyone inside! Unshaken, the young woman stepped out through the castle gate to face her opponent.

She looked out across the clearing to the edge of the forest at the foothills of the mountain. Sure enough, there stood an enormous giant! For a moment, she just stood and stared at him from a distance. There was a gentle rise in the ground separating the two, so she could only see him from the waist up. It was difficult to tell exactly how big he was, but he was clearly taller than any man she had seen or heard of. She was struck with the same awe and terror all her predecessors surely felt at that moment. The giant was real. And facing him today, she would surely die. She considered running back inside the castle walls. But she had given her word to the good people inside to face their giant. So, with all the bravery she could muster, she began to walk tentatively toward the giant. And the giant began to walk toward her.

After a few paces up the gentle incline, she gained full line of sight, and could see his whole form. With the better angle, she could tell he was not nearly the 10 feet in height she first believed, but perhaps only 7 feet tall. He was still massive, but at least now in human proportions. She was still no match for him, but at least she would meet her defeat at the hands of something recognizable.

With that element of the unknown removed, she could walk at a normal pace. And after a few more steps, the giant appeared to be smaller still. Was this some strange optical illusion? The giant appeared to be not much bigger than she was now. She might actually have a fighting chance! With this new hope, her pace quickened. And with every step she could tell it was no illusion. The giant was shrinking before her very eyes, and the faster she ran, the faster the giant shrank.

Her terror had turned to hope, and now that hope had turned to confidence. Certain of her victory, she was now in an all-out sprint toward the giant. As she reached the middle of the clearing she stopped and stood toe to toe with the giant, who was now 12 inches tall and still shrinking quickly. She reached down and picked him up in the palm of her hand. She only had time to ask him one question before he shrank down to the size of a grain of sand and blew away in the next gust of wind.

"Who are you?" she asked earnestly.

The giant responded in a tiny and dwindling voice, "I am known by many names. To the Chinese, I am *kongju*. To the Greeks, I am *phobos*. But to your people, brave one, I am known simply as fear."

She had come to the village to learn something. And indeed, she had. If you face your fears and confront them with confidence, they will shrink before your very eyes.

As I read this story, it was clear how the girl faced her fears. She ran at the fear with action. She had some second guessing, but kept taking action. The fear turned into hope, and then the hope turned into confidence. As I think about the fears we have about our business, it is best to simply face those fears. Keep doing what you need to do to be successful. Do not stand still, but take action toward your goals. Don't let the numbers scare you, but embrace them because the path will become more clear as you move toward the fear of the unknown.

5 Ways to Embrace Your Fears

1. Develop an action plan and follow it.

2. Review the numbers regularly. It is easier in small chunks.

3. Remember why you are in business.

4. Visualize a better future.

5. Ask for guidance and courage – from God and others.

Call to Clarity

Think of one thing you fear regarding your business finances. How can you embrace this fear and be courageous?

CHAPTER 4

10 WAYS BUSINESSES ACT LIKE A TEENAGER

Having teenagers of my own, I have noticed some striking similarities between how they operate and how struggling businesses often operate. As we continue to assess where we are today in our businesses, let's see if any of the issues below are challenges you face.

1. Impulsive Decision-Making

Some business owners tend to make decisions by their gut without much strategic or financial analysis. I don't recommend getting stuck in "analysis paralysis," but there should be some basis for decision making. Mindtools.com recommends the following approach:

- Create a constructive environment.
- Investigate the situation in detail.
- Generate good alternatives.
- Explore your options.
- Select the best solution.

- Evaluate your plan.

- Communicate your decision and take action.

I have always been a fan of Pro/Con lists, and in the book *Creating Great Choices*, the authors mention creating a Pro/Pro list. When we start with negatives, there is a tendency to shut down the consideration of the choice. We can start to not take this choice seriously. In reality, many times one negative is a positive for the other choice. We are usually looking at a third approach that takes the best of both alternatives.

2. Difficulty Delaying Gratification

My teenager cannot save money for long. He earns money from doing chores and mowing the lawn, but he is in debt quite often and spends money on food and entertainment regularly. Many times, he regrets how he has spent his money. Once, he was upset that he paid $5.00 for a movie on Itunes instead of going to Red Box and paying $1.50. I recommended that he have a budget. I know you might find this humorous, but if he can learn the lesson now, how much better will it be later when he has a much larger budget?

Businesses should have a budget, approval system, and a process for reviewing actual expenses to the budget. This will not only help in delaying gratification, but the plan will make decisions so much easier.

3. Making Excuses Instead of Taking Responsibility

My teenage son rarely takes responsibility for anything. Somehow very little is ever his fault. I know that we can all fall into this trap, but no matter the challenge a business is facing, we can all take responsibility to improve the situation.

There are many unforeseen events that are outside of our control, but if we are honest with ourselves, we are in control of more than we think. Certainly, we are in control of our reaction, focus, and ability to learn from mistakes.

4. Procrastination

I know all of us have waited until the last minute to do something. Many of us believe that our best work is done when the pressure is on. The fact remains that adequate planning is always more effective and leads to less stress and increased creativity. If you need the sense of pressure, try developing internal mini-deadlines to help achieve a larger goal.

5. Arguing About Everything

Maybe it is a teenager's desire for independence, but they tend to argue about everything (at least mine does). Similarly, businesses tend to have silos between departments and levels of experience that can cause a spirit of disagreement. Large businesses call this bureaucracy, but even a small business can have dysfunctional politics that slow down the growth of the organization.

6. Don't like Change

Kids and teenagers tend to like everything to remain the same. Most adults are very averse to change, and I admit to falling into this category sometimes. One thing is certain: change will happen, so we should embrace it.

Change is a law of life. And those who only look to the past or present are certain to miss the future. - John F. Kennedy.

7. Emotionally Inconsistent

We all know that pre-teens and teenagers can be emotionally unstable, and it is challenging to know how they are going to react to different situations. Leaders of a business must be consistent in their communication and reaction. How they treat different employees should be the same no matter their mood or stress level. This is hard, of course, but necessary.

8. Lack of Empathy

I truly believe the empathy portion of a teenager's brain has not been fully developed. It can be challenging for them to think of anyone else besides themselves. Let's face it, we are all selfish to certain degrees, but we have to be careful and learn to be empathetic to other viewpoints in the organization. Obviously, we can't please everyone, but the act of listening and considering different viewpoints will go a long way towards getting people to work together.

9. Manipulation

Manipulation seems to be learned at an early age. I have seen one of my kids trying to pit my wife and me against each other sometimes through effective and well-thought out manipulation. He might not really know he is doing it. He wants to get his way and will do whatever it takes to get it.

I know this is prevalent in businesses. The problem is that it breaks down communication and causes infighting and lowers morale. The productivity of the employees will decrease, and people will feel like there is an unfair system. This will lead to lower employee retention, which is not good for growth.

10. Short-Term Mindset

It is very hard for many teenagers to think far down the road. They have a short-term view of life. Businesses cannot operate this way. Yes, they need to be flexible, but they should have a strategic vision and plan. They should communicate the goals and plan to help them meet those goals.

Most people overestimate what they can do in one year and underestimate what they can do in ten years. – Bill Gates

Do any of these resonate with you? Think of at least one that you want to improve in your business. Let's develop an abundant and empowering mindset and move into adulthood to experience the growth that comes along with it.

Call to Clarity

Of the 10 issues mentioned in this chapter, which one resonates with you? How might you keep yourself from falling into this trap?

CHAPTER 5

DEVELOPING AN ABUNDANCE MINDSET THROUGH LIFE'S CHANGES

I did not want to move my home office. I had started my new business in that office and was comfortable there. I purchased a new office door and spent all Christmas Eve installing it. I added foam around the door frame. I spent hours trying to get the door to shut correctly. After $150 and 10 hours, I came to a sad realization: the sound proofing didn't work. Then, I searched online for other solutions and found that they would be a lot of work and time.

I needed to cut my losses. I had to accept the idea that I should move my office upstairs. It seemed like so much work. Finally, I dove in. I found that when I am working, it doesn't seem so bad. When I step back and start dwelling on all the work, it is overwhelming. I got my wife and kids to help. Even my 4-year-old niece and 7-year old nephew were here, and they helped.

We spent hours breaking down the treadmill without the proper tools, but through sheer determination we got it out of the room. Heavy furniture needed to be broken apart, moved, and then put back together. My wife even called a neighbor to help me move a heavy filing cabinet.

The project took time, but once we got started, there was no looking back. We certainly weren't going to move everything again and go back to the way it was.

So why do I bring this up for an abundance mindset? Let's consider what happened and how it relates to a business.

1. In business, we should try things and keep plugging away until we figure out how to make it work.

2. Sometimes we have to cut our losses and listen to others' advice. Yes, my wife wanted me to move my office upstairs, but I was stubborn and kept saying something about preferring taller ceilings and other excuses.

3. Change is hard, and it is a lot of work before it gets better. It does get better. Sometimes it is two steps forward and one step back. In the end, though, better processes, people, and products do result in higher profit.

Change is the heartbeat of growth. - Scottie Somers

Change is hard at first, messy in the middle and gorgeous at the end. - Robin Sharma

Life is Change. Growth is optional. - John Maxwell

The world hates change, yet it is the only thing that has brought progress. - Charles Kettering

If there is no struggle, there is no progress. - Frederick Douglass

One of the challenges I have found in both business and life is to determine when a change needs to be made. When is changing a good thing? When is changing not so good? As a business grows, change is inevitable, and it is important to have the systems and processes to handle it. The same is important in life spiritually, intellectually, physically, and emotionally.

My career in finance and accounting has been full of change. New systems, reports, processes, acquisitions, promotions, new jobs, and now my own business have all brought change for me at various points. Sometimes I have held on too long to familiarity, and sometimes I took the leap.

Below are five ways in which change is good.

1. Improvement & Growth

As a business increases transactions, revenue, and employees, there has to be a change in processes, finance, cash flow, and reports. Whenever a system is implemented that will allow for scalable growth in an organization, change is good. It can be hard to implement a new accounting system or create a new billing system, but in the end, it is worth it. In all situations, there is always more work before it becomes less work.

Reading, learning something new, implementing a new process, or accepting new ideas is challenging, but it always leads to growth.

2. Future View

Developing a life plan is essential to have a future view of living. Even though we want to be present in our life, we need to think about where we want to be next year, 3 years, or even 5 years from now. It is very effective to write this down in a Life Plan and review and adjust on a regular basis. Check out the book *Living Forward* for more help on this.

Before making a change, think about how this change could result in something better in the future. Starting a business with a well-documented plan can be a positive change if it leads to doing the work you love and to securing more financial freedom. Hiring for a new position is scary at first, but it can be positive if it puts your business in a place to be more competitive, grow revenues, and to have more influence in the marketplace.

The key is that there is a long-term vision to see the end. "Begin with the end in mind" is one of the habits Stephen Covey writes about in *7 Habits of Highly Effective People*.

3. Optimism

Any change that has a negative view might not be the right kind of change. What is a negative view? I am thinking that you are changing only because a competitor is doing it, but you go into it with pessimism. Any change needs to be thought of as eventually being positive. If the people in the organization are negative, resentful, or uncooperative, change will not work. Focusing on the improvement, growth, and the positive future of the business will lead to optimism and can help with change management.

4. Peace

Any change made out of revenge, anger, frustration, or fear is usually not good change. This is the hardest one for me to tell the difference. Change in and of itself is scary and not peaceful. How do we have peace when change is not peaceful? In my life, I rely on prayer, in meditation on God's Word (the Bible), and journaling.

Journaling helps deflate some of the emotion and helps us be more logical. I have guys that keep me accountable whom I go to when I need to process decisions and information.

Sometimes talking it out with a friend, mentor, or leader in the organization can make all the difference and bring peace.

5. Abundance

Change is easier when we have an abundance mindset which is that resources, money, opportunities, and business are continually increasing. The alternative is the view is scarcity in that there is only a certain amount of opportunity out there and that we are all trying to get a piece of it. I believe in abundance. Technological advances are happening all the time. We can always learn something new and be more efficient with our time. Good change leads to abundance.

We all know that change is going to happen, so we must look for ways to embrace it through personal development and growth. When we have a future-oriented mindset, the change will get more exciting. Staying optimistic and having peace about the change will result in abundance in the long-term.

Call to Clarity

Do you embrace change easily? Which of the five good reasons for change is the most motivating and why?

CHAPTER 6

COMMON SMALL BUSINESS QUESTIONS

In meeting with various business owners, there are many common financial concerns. Very few if any have ever asked me for a business model to help make better financial decisions. They have concerns that are phrased a bit differently. Below are five financial desires of business owners. Have you said any of these?

1. "I want to know where my cash is going."

Do you make decisions by looking at your bank account? Do you wonder how you are always out of money, but you are working so hard and bringing in more and more revenue?

When I was a teenager, we had a dry erase board in our kitchen where we would write funny quotes. Do you remember the quotes on *Saturday Night Live* from Jack Handey in the 1990s? They were written in a profound way but were very obvious. We would try to write quotes like this. One time my older brother who was probably 16 years old simply put "Money goes away." He had noticed that even when you seem to have a lot of money, it can disappear without much thought. You are suddenly left wondering what happened.

2. "I want to pay Uncle Sam less."

Nobody wants to pay more taxes. I spoke with a potential client who said that his main concern was paying less in taxes. He only had a paper checkbook as a financial record, it would be rather time-consuming to understand his financial situation quickly. No matter how small or large, any kind of tax planning would require a forecast. You have to understand your potential revenue, profit, and cash flow to understand ways to best reduce your tax liability.

3. "I want to have more peace and less stress financially."

Don't we all want more peace? Financial stress is debilitating. If you are in financial stress, you know you need to spend money, but don't have the money or cash to spend. When we are stressed, we must take action. What action do we take? It is best if the action is coordinated toward a specific goal. Your financial goal will be developed in a forecast model for your business. The knowledge and understanding that your actions are moving you toward a financial goal can make things less stressful.

4. "I want to know when I can hire an employee or contractor."

Eventually, any business gets to the size where you will need contractors or eventually employees to truly grow. When can you afford to hire someone? Most people look at the workload and hire when they feel they need it. Unfortunately, feelings can lie to you. What happens if the employee takes more time to get up to speed than you thought? Can you go 90-180 days without much productivity from your employees? Do you have the cash to last that long? Many times, it is best to start with a contractor and work up to employees. A financial model will help with this kind of analysis.

5. "Do I need to borrow or get an investor?"

It seems common for a entrepreneur to think they need to borrow money to start a business. I worked for a business and started my own with no debt. I do agree that having some savings is very helpful, but you don't always need to borrow money or to get investors. Now, in some cases this is necessary. It really does depend on what business you are starting. A forecasting model will help you decide not only if you need to borrow or raise the capital, but it will also tell you how much money you need.

We all desire the same final result: more cash now and to pay less taxes. We want more peace and to sleep better. Also, we want our business to grow faster or to get help from employees that are ready to go on day one. It could be that we are impatient and don't have time for all the steps, but we have to follow the steps. As we walk down the trail of business ownership, there are steps we must take to reach the destination we desire.

The first step to answering these questions is to know where you are today, but there is more to it. You desire to get to a destination in your business. You want increasing revenue, profits, and cash flow. This is where mapping out your financial destination is essential.

In the next part, we will go through the journey of mapping out this destination by discussing the best way to go about it. It is the journey that is the adventure. The answers will become clearer as we go.

Call to Clarity

What is one financial issue you want to solve in your business?

PART 2

DETERMINE YOUR DESTINATION

We should now consider the destination and how long it will take to get there. Time and money are two essential variables. Most businesses desire to grow each year, but how fast should they grow? I have talked to business owners who want to double their revenue in one year. Then, they say they want to triple their revenue. Never mind that these are aggressive goals, but this mindset causes a change in destination. More growth will typically require more cash, personnel, and processes to reach your new goal.

We must be clear on a reasonable but challenging goal, with a plan for success. We should have the people, processes, profits, and even products to get us to this destination. One valuable tool is to build a financial forecasting model to show the clients, expenses, people, and all the variables necessary to achieve these goals.

In this section, we will discuss how to build a model that you can use to get to the destination you desire in your business. We will start by examining revenue, assessing expenses, and then calculating possible profits which leads to cash flow projections. Different decisions lead to different results.

CHAPTER 7

TO PLAN OR NOT TO PLAN

In reading the book *Anything You Want: 40 Lessons for a New Kind of Entrepreneur*, I came across a chapter titled, "You don't need a plan or vision." What is the author, Derek Sivers, talking about? Did I read this right? What about the following quotes?

By failing to prepare, you are preparing to fail. - Benjamin Franklin

In preparing for battle, I have always found that plans are useless, but planning is indispensable. - Dwight Eisenhower

Plans are of little importance, but planning is essential. - Winston Churchill

The basic point of this chapter is that when Sivers put a plan together for his business, CD Baby, he thought that one day he could have 1,000 artists on the site and would eventually need to hire a 3rd employee. Years later when he had over 100,000 artists selling CDs on their site and 85 employees, he made fun of this forecast with his business partner.

Here are some thoughts to keep us from going down the wrong path.

1. Don't go to Extremes

It is easy for analytical and financial types to put together complicated spreadsheets and models that very few people can understand. I had one sent to me that would have taken me a day to figure out where all the cells were linked. I do think this is overboard. In some cases, it is required if you are trying to raise venture capital, but I do think it can lead to analysis paralysis.

On the other hand, one of my clients mentioned in a speech that their organization had never had plans since the beginning, but they survived. I am not sure if he was claiming this was good or bad but they were in need of financial help.

2. Planning is Different than a Plan

A plan is a document that is set in stone and put on a shelf and nobody looks at it. The best method is to develop a forecast that is updated regularly. My favorite analogy is the weather forecast. You would not look at the forecast from a week ago and rely on it for today. The best forecast for today is actually last night or maybe this morning. The data is changing and so is your forecast.

I know that forecasting the weather seems inaccurate. But in reality, meteorology has improved greatly in the last few years. Meteorologists are better than ever at predicting one or two days out, in part due to their increased ability to accurately assess data over longer time periods to achieve model consistency. Your business is the same. The more consistent financial data you have over a longer period, the less often you will experience financial surprises. This improves your ability to make effective, confident decisions in your own business.

Predicting the weather forecast without knowing the current conditions is pretty useless. A meteorologist must track temperature, humidity, wind speed, and other important current metrics. Your business requires similar metrics that must be measured currently that are unique to your own business. When weather forecasters see that the current situation is not in line with their previous forecast models, they are required to update their projection based on current trending. If the forecast predicted a 60 percent chance of snow, and it is now currently snowing, you can bet they will be updating their forecast based on current conditions. The same concept applies to your business.

Let's not confuse planning. Forecasts are often wrong, but the act of doing the plan is what makes all the difference.

3. Exaggeration vs. Reality

Sometimes, book and chapter titles are meant to exaggerate so people will read them. In reality, Derek Sivers did have some planning and some metrics that were used to run his business. Yes, they were short term and it worked for him. For example, he had to determine how much to charge the music artists who sold CDs on his site. He did some research. The reality was a bit different than the title of the chapter.

We all hear stories of people with no plans who became successful, and it seems like it all fell into their laps. I do think this happens sometimes, but rarely. Most of the time, if you search deeper, you find that the person who is successful worked very hard and tried many different things before it looked like it "fell into their lap."

In summary, I am still going to talk about the importance of planning for success in your business. There is a lot of great information in Derek Sivers' book, so I recommend you pick it up.

Call to Clarity

Do you plan too much or too little? What adjustments are needed so that you can begin measuring your business results against expectations?

CHAPTER 8

IT ALL STARTS WITH REVENUE

I had the privilege to work as a Controller of a small start-up digital marketing company starting in 2005. Looking back, the company was made up of strong leaders, entrepreneurs, and visionaries. I remember one time in 2007 when we had lost five of the top ten clients and we needed to make up the revenue. We determined that we needed about $500,000 additional revenue to hit the goal for the year, and it was September.

The company president spoke to everyone and let them know the revenue shortfall that was needed in order to hit the annual goal and get bonuses. We broke the goal down to $10,000 per employee and gave everyone individual goals. It seemed much more achievable when broken down by employee and month.

The employees were inspired and were nimble and flexible to make quick adjustments by offering new services and innovative ideas to existing clients. In fact, we came up with innovative ways to upsell and improve services. We ended up shattering the goal. We also were in position for excellent growth the following year.

Do you have an organized approach to forecast your revenue?

Have you looked at your revenue projections for the next year? Do you know how to do this?

The very first step in building a financial model for your business, or any organization for that matter, is to have a revenue plan. Where is your income coming from? Why should you do this?

Below are five reasons this is important:

- Gaining a better understanding of your revenue potential builds excitement.

- Measurable goals are more likely to be accomplished.

- Revenue is the key to forecasting your profit, and ultimately, cash flow.

- Revenue builds momentum which breeds success.

- A revenue plan helps you focus and prioritize on all your opportunities.

So now that you are convinced, here are the steps to accomplish this:

1. Understand Your Existing Revenue

You will need spreadsheet software such as Microsoft Excel, Google Sheets, or Numbers to do this.

List all your clients, products/services, and future months in different columns.

Forecast your projected revenue based on what is currently contracted by month for at least 12 months or the end of the next fiscal year.

Assume business-as-usual to forecast beyond the contract term.

Total all the months and full 12 months for each row.

Figure 8.1: Revenue by Existing Client and Service Forecast

Client	Service	Jan-XX	Feb-XX	Mar-XX	Apr-XX	May-XX	Jun-XX	Jul-XX	Aug-XX	Sep-XX	Oct-XX	Nov-XX	Dec-XX	Total 20XX
Client A	Service 1	5,000	5,000	5,000	5,000	5,000	5,000	5,000	5,000	5,000	5,000	5,000	5,000	60,000
Client A	Service 2	6,000	6,000	6,000	6,000	6,000	6,000	6,000	6,000	6,000	6,000	6,000	6,000	72,000
Client A	Service 3	2,000	2,000	2,000	2,000	2,000	2,000	2,000	2,000	2,000	2,000	2,000	2,000	24,000
Client B	Service 1	1,000	1,000	1,000	1,000	1,000	1,000	1,000	1,000	1,000	1,000	1,000	1,000	12,000
Client B	Service 2	2,000	2,000	2,000	2,000	2,000	2,000	2,000	2,000	2,000	2,000	2,000	2,000	24,000
Client B	Service 3	2,000	2,000	2,000	2,000	2,000	2,000	2,000	2,000	2,000	2,000	2,000	2,000	24,000
Client C	Service 1	3,000	3,000	3,000	3,000	3,000	3,000	3,000	3,000	3,000	3,000	3,000	3,000	36,000
Client C	Service 2	1,400	1,400	1,400	1,400	1,400	1,400	1,400	1,400	1,400	1,400	1,400	1,400	16,800
Client C	Service 3	200	200	200	200	200	200	200	200	200	200	200	200	2,400
Total Existing Revenue		22,600	22,600	22,600	22,600	22,600	22,600	22,600	22,600	22,600	22,600	22,600	22,600	271,200

For physical products, list the average quantity, price, and sales in different rows to calculate potential sales. Trend quantity, price, and sales based on the last few months or last year at the same time if you are in a seasonal industry.

Figure 8.2: Revenue by Product and Quantity Forecast

Client	Product		Jan-XX	Feb-XX	Mar-XX	Apr-XX	May-XX	Jun-XX	Jul-XX	Aug-XX	Sep-XX	Oct-XX	Nov-XX	Dec-XX	Total 20XX
		Qty	50	55	60	65	65	70	80	90	100	100	110	110	
		Price	$ 20	$ 20	$ 20	$ 20	$ 20	$ 20	$ 20	$ 20	$ 20	$ 20	$ 20	$ 20	
Client A	Product 1	Sales	$1,000	$1,100	$1,200	$1,300	$1,300	$1,400	$1,600	$1,800	$2,000	$2,000	$2,200	$2,200	$ 19,100
		Qty	15	20	25	30	35	40	45	50	55	60	65	70	
		Price	$ 100	$ 100	$ 100	$ 100	$ 100	$ 100	$ 100	$ 100	$ 100	$ 100	$ 100	$ 100	
Client A	Product 2	Sales	$1,500	$2,000	$2,500	$3,000	$3,500	$4,000	$4,500	$5,000	$5,500	$6,000	$6,500	$7,000	$ 51,000
		Qty	5	5	7	9	10	12	13	15	15	18	20	20	
		Price	$ 297	$ 297	$ 297	$ 297	$ 297	$ 297	$ 297	$ 297	$ 297	$ 297	$ 297	$ 297	
Client B	Product 2	Sales	$1,485	$1,485	$2,079	$2,673	$2,970	$3,564	$3,861	$4,455	$4,455	$5,346	$5,940	$5,940	$ 44,253
Total Existing Revenue			3,985	4,585	5,779	6,973	7,770	8,964	9,961	11,255	11,955	13,346	14,640	15,140	114,353

2. New Revenue Opportunities from Existing Clients

It is very important to consider all revenue opportunities from existing clients. They are the quickest way to grow your revenue plan. I remember when working at a digital marketing agency that the revenue growth from existing clients, year-over-year, was over 50% in many years. Some clients go away, but the ones that stick with you will grow if you are adding the value that is necessary to keep them with you for the long-term. Create a chart like the first one above, but add a column for probability and another for annual revenue.

See below for an example. Also, add any new services that are being launched.

So how do you decide on the probability of closing new revenue from existing clients? I would use 25%, 50%, 75%, and 90% probability to decide.

- 25% is for opportunities that you just started discussing.

- 50% is for revenue from services you have pitched where there is significant interest.

- 75% if there is a verbal commitment, but the timing may still be unclear.

- 90% if you have sent a contract and are awaiting signature.

The key is to review all possibilities on a regular basis. When you approach your clients with other services and products, it shows that you desire to add value to their business, which is valuable in and of itself.

Figure 8.3: Potential New Revenue by Client, Prospect, and Service Forecast

Client	Service	Annual Revenue	Probability	Jan-XX	Feb-XX	Mar-XX	Apr-XX	May-XX	Jun-XX	Jul-XX	Aug-XX	Sep-XX	Oct-XX	Nov-XX	Dec-XX	Total 20XX
Client A	Service 1	$ 100,000	50%	4,167	4,167	4,167	4,167	4,167	4,167	4,167	4,167	4,167	4,167	4,167	4,167	50,000
Client A	Service 2	$ 50,000	25%	1,042	1,042	1,042	1,042	1,042	1,042	1,042	1,042	1,042	1,042	1,042	1,042	12,500
Client A	Service 3	$ 25,000	75%	1,563	1,563	1,563	1,563	1,563	1,563	1,563	1,563	1,563	1,563	1,563	1,563	18,750
Client B	Service 1	$ 30,000	50%	1,250	1,250	1,250	1,250	1,250	1,250	1,250	1,250	1,250	1,250	1,250	1,250	15,000
Client B	Service 2	$ 10,000	50%	417	417	417	417	417	417	417	417	417	417	417	417	5,000
Client B	Service 3	$ 10,000	50%	417	417	417	417	417	417	417	417	417	417	417	417	5,000
Prospect 1	Service 1	$ 100,000	75%	6,250	6,250	6,250	6,250	6,250	6,250	6,250	6,250	6,250	6,250	6,250	6,250	75,000
Prospect 1	Service 2	$ 50,000	25%	1,042	1,042	1,042	1,042	1,042	1,042	1,042	1,042	1,042	1,042	1,042	1,042	12,500
Prospect 1	Service 3	$ 50,000	25%	1,042	1,042	1,042	1,042	1,042	1,042	1,042	1,042	1,042	1,042	1,042	1,042	12,500
Total Existing Revenue		$425,000		17,188	17,188	17,188	17,188	17,188	17,188	17,188	17,188	17,188	17,188	17,188	17,188	206,250

This approach can be used for products rather than services. You may adjust quantities or price also, if that is a possibility.

3. New Revenue from Prospects

We should all be looking for revenue from prospects if we desire to grow. Once you start having a conversation in which there is realistic interest, you should add this prospect to the new revenue report. Some people call this a "sales pipeline". Once again you are going to assess the probability to getting the new business.

For those who sell tangible products, you have to consider variables such as quantity, price, and product margin. You may have many customers, so it isn't feasible to list all of them. You might group them by region or target market. At least have a category for new customers and assign a probability for all products.

In summary, forecasting revenue is essential for the success of your business. First, understand how your existing clients, services, and products are trending for the next 12 months. Second, consider all the ways you can add more value to your existing clients through new services and products and forecast that revenue by probability. Finally, list out all of your prospects and assign a probability based on where they are in the sales cycle.

Once you have completed your existing revenue and new revenue forecasts, you can look more closely at expenses and profit.

Do you have a revenue plan for the next 12 months? Take some time to review your existing customers' revenue and prospects to understand your potential. Don't be surprised at the results. The additional clarity is essential for your strategic growth.

For more guidance with building the revenue forecast, please see Appendix 1 – Mechanics of the Forecast Model.

Call to Clarity

Have you built a prospecting plan? If so, review and update it and schedule time to do this on a regular basis. If not, get started today because this may be the most important exercise that can build clarity in your business.

CHAPTER 9

HOW TO SPEND WISELY

We live in a world in which we always want more. We spend more, we want more revenue or income, and then we spend more. Many of us buy cars, go on vacations, and we work to spend our way to happiness.

A *UBS Investor Watch* article has some interesting facts about the aspirations and desires of millionaires. Fifty-eight percent of millionaires say they have an increasing standard of living. Sixty-four percent say their living expectations have gone up. Those with one million dollars want two million and those with ten million want twenty-five million. They have an increasing fear of losing their money. Nearly half of GenX and Millennial millionaires (those born 1965 to 1995) fear the loss of their wealth and feel pressure to keep up with others.

We could have a whole discussion about wealth, abundance, and fear. The point I really want to make is that it seems the more people make, the more they spend. This means that if you are a business owner, then revenue might solve your problems in the short term, but eventually, expenses will catch up without some control.

I believe any business should work to grow revenue consistently, but that alone will not make you profitable. We must be smart with our expenses and ensure we have the profit we desire.

Why are You a Business Owner?

Ask yourself why you have a business. Why do you want to grow your business? Surely you don't want to grow revenue with no profits or cash to show for it. I am not referring to businesses that are taking on venture capital investment with losses for years to gain market share or launch a new product that has not yet hit critical mass (ex. Facebook or Amazon in their early years).

Maybe you started your business because you saw a need in the marketplace, and you want to provide a service or product to meet that need. Or maybe you want to build a business that has value. What about having the freedom to grow your business the way you see best? You could want to give your family a tangible money generating business that provides a great service to others. Maybe you want to have multiple revenue streams which provide more security in the long run than a job. As a general rule, business ownership is a better way to build wealth than being an employee.

There could be other reasons why you started your own business. Understanding your "why" of being a business owner is essential to making sure you stay on track.

Key Expense Categories

Below is a list of main expense categories that all business owners should understand and manage.

Cost of Goods or Services

If you sell a tangible product, cost of goods could be materials, labor, and/or shipping costs. If you sell a service, you might hire others to perform some of the services. You want to know your gross margin. The Gross Margin percentage [(Sales − Cost of Goods / Services Sold) / Sales] varies by industry. In a high services or software business, it could be over 70%. For a tangible product business, it could be 20% − 50%. Obviously, you want higher margin within reason. You need to find a way to streamline and differentiate yourself to grow margin without losing business to competitors.

Personnel (Salaries, payroll taxes, fringe benefits)

When can you hire? What is the fully loaded expense for an employee? Also, when do you use a contractor, and when do you hire?

There is the target allocation percent approach. This means that you want your Personnel expenses to stay at, for example, 30% of your revenue or some percentage that you see fit. Be sure to account not only for salary expenses, but also for bonuses, payroll taxes, insurance expenses, retirement, and any other fringe benefits.

There is the Revenue by Person approach. I used this regularly at an online marketing agency. Basically, we determined how much revenue per employee per month required to get the margins we desired. When revenue grew, then we hired accordingly.

Advertising and Marketing

Advertising and Marketing are essential for the survival of any business. This includes some of the following:

- Business Cards and Brochures

- Your website and social media channel

- Paid online advertising

- Conferences and trade shows

- Advertisements on billboards, radio, magazines, television, newspapers, etc.

- Content creation such as e-books, white papers, presentations, webinars, free courses

- Networking organization fees (Professional organizations, Chambers)

I am sure there are more areas, but I included the ones that are most prevalent.

How much do you spend here? I would say you spend as much as you can, but still leave yourself with some sort of operating profit. If you are just starting out, you might want to consider spending as much as possible here after paying yourself. I know I had to dip into my savings to build a website and start networking.

Training & Development

In this day of change, we have to continuously improve ourselves. I have heard that we should spend 3-5% of our revenue on training and development. If we apply what we have learned, then we will receive benefits many times our investment.

Some ideas for training could be podcasts, books, online courses, conferences, classes, and business coaching.

Travel Expenses

Travel expenses may be necessary to visit clients or attend conferences. These expenses include airfare, hotels, meals, entertainment, taxis, mileage, parking, tolls, etc.

Planning out the number of employees and trips in advance will help you stay on top of this. It is usually cheaper to book everything a few weeks in advance to get the best deal. If you have many employees, you should have a travel and expense policy to make it clear what can be reimbursed. Consider using expense reimbursement software such as Expensify to help streamline online expense reporting, approval, and reimbursement processes.

Equipment, Office, and Facilities

Office rent, utilities, and maintenance expenses can be significant. It is important to understand how these expenses change as you add staff or equipment. Equipment or vehicle expenses such as fuel, repairs, and maintenance increase as they get older. It can be valuable to do a purchase versus a lease analysis as there are many options to consider that affect performance, down time, expenses, and cash flow.

You might have other expenses, but I have hit on the big ones. Overall, after you have deducted expenses from revenue, you desire an operating profit that is healthy. You want to get operating margin to 20% or more. This is different by industry, but 20-30% will allow you to build a business that becomes more valuable. You will be able to explore new products and services. It will allow you to be more flexible and nimble as the economy and industry change.

"You can't grow out of your profit problem. You need to fix profit first, then grow." -Mike Michalowicz from his book *Profit First*

Expense management might not be as exciting as revenue, but it is essential for profitability.

For more guidance on expense forecasting, check out Appendix 1 – Mechanics of the Forecast Model.

Call to Clarity

Do you know your current monthly recurring expenses? If not, I suggest finding a bookkeeper to help you get organized.

CHAPTER 10

WAYS TO FOCUS ON PROFITS

As a business owner, do you feel you are not getting paid what you are worth? Have you not taken a profit distribution in years or do you not even know what a profit distribution is? Do you dread tax time because you do not have enough to pay your taxes regularly? Have you bought into the lie that that best way to grow your business is through bank loans or investors?

If your answer is "Yes" to any of these questions, then I recommend an intentional focus on Profit.

Below are five ways to focus on profits.

1. Know Your Financials

Business owners should have a basic understanding of their Income Statement, Balance Sheet, and Cash Flow. I realize that this is easier said than done in most cases. My goal is to work to educate business owners on how to do this and why. The biggest challenge is having current financials. Most accounting software will generate these reports. A good accountant or bookkeeper can help ensure this is happening. The financials will not mean much unless you compare to something useful. At the very least, understanding revenue, expense, profit, and cash flow compared to last year, budget, and the monthly trend will be a great starting place. Ensure you have this within a few weeks of the prior month so that the information will have some value to you.

Do not rely on year-end tax accounting to know your financials. This is way too late and does not give you time to make any meaningful changes.

2. Routine Checks

Regular meetings to check your financials should be scheduled. Meet with your key personnel to discuss what is happening to trends. By having monthly or at least quarterly meetings, you can establish a routine of financial success and metrics. The hardest part, at times, is establishing a benchmark for meaningful information. It is similar to attending a sporting event and not knowing how the score is kept. Obviously, the score in golf is different than in bowling. Try understanding tennis, or even cricket, without prior knowledge.

Once you have a basic understanding of revenue, gross and operating margin, and profit, you can better see if you are improving. If you aren't saving any cash for taxes, bonuses, distributions, inventory, or property and equipment, you could be in trouble. That leads me to *Profit First*.

3. The *Profit First* Dashboard

Mike Michalowicz's book *Profit First* is an important read for anyone leading a business or working with business owners. He recommends opening separate bank accounts for Profit, Revenue, Taxes, Operating Expenses, and Owner's Compensation/Payroll. Additionally, he suggests opening a Profit Hold and Tax Hold Savings account at another bank and keeping it out of sight. Each quarter, you take half the money from the Profit Hold account for a profit distribution.

Of course, the Tax Hold account is to pay quarterly taxes and to ensure you have enough for annual taxes.

The reason why I think this is an ingenious idea is because it gives you a daily cash dashboard through bank accounts. You know where you stand and how much to spend for Payroll and Operating Expenses. You can even open other accounts for Inventory, Equipment, or possibly Reimbursable Expenses. Now, at first this does seem like quite a few bank accounts. I would suggest getting a bookkeeper to help you manage the cash flow. Once the system is in place, the owners can login to their bank accounts and know exactly where they stand regarding profit, revenue, and key expense categories.

Warning: This type of dashboard does not work for all business owners such as those that heavily utilize credit cards or debt to fund their business. In this case, up-to-date financials and a good accountant can help.

4. Plan for Success

A working business plan is essential for success. I am not talking about a business plan that you might create for an investor or bank and then never look at it again. I am talking about the plan that is used every day for your business. This plan shows revenue by customer, product, and month. It also shows potential revenue for closing prospects or launching new products. The plan forecasts your potential expenses, hiring, profits, and cash flow. The plan gives you a goal to reach that is reasonable.

This working plan allows you to understand the financial impact of new business or not getting new business. It allows for quick decisions on what you can afford and what you should avoid. It saves you time and builds the organization. My favorite result is that it decreases chaos which is expensive, time-consuming, and nerve-wracking.

5. Value Your Time

I can't really talk about profit without talking about time. Of course, you know time is money, right? The hardest part for entrepreneurs and business owners is to let things go that others can do. If you are doing something that you can pay someone $20 an hour to do, then why don't you delegate it? Most business owners are probably worth $100-$500 per hour depending on the size of their organization. The more time you spend on the previous four ways to increase profit will be valuable and will itself increase profits. You have to be strategic, focus on business and product development, and train your team.

Top 5 Places to Save Money in Your Business

There are many ways to become a more profitable business. Revenue growth is essential and updating processes to increase productivity is important. My favorite way to add value and increase profit is simply to review expenses. It doesn't matter if you are a small business, solopreneur, or large enterprise. A regular review of expenses is essential to success.

We create value by increasing profit (increase revenue, decrease expenses), saving time, or increasing impact. It does take some time to review expenses, but saving expenses adds up over time.

Below are five areas to focus on when reviewing expenses.

1. Credit Card Processing Fees

One client of mine was paying interchange plus 1.25% for all credit/debit charges. Over time, the bank had increased fees slowly. After a little shopping around, we switched credit card processors, and the fees dropped to interchange plus 0.10%, which saved my client $15,000 annually.

There are many credit card processors, so review your options. More and more transactions are paid via credit card, so savings can add up over time.

2. Business Insurance

Property, General Liability, Workers Compensation, and Auto Insurance providers should be evaluated on a regular basis. Sometimes, it even helps to have another broker shop the insurance every couple of years. I have seen some cases where the property was over insured, which resulted in thousands of extra dollars spent on premiums. Workers Compensation can be too high if forms are completed incorrectly by employee classification. There are so many people who can help in this area that it is not hard to shop this around.

3. Software Subscription Costs

Since software has become more cloud-based, almost all software is charged as a recurring monthly fee. The problem comes when you stop using a particular software. The software vendor has your card information and will keep charging you until eternity. In larger businesses, the accounting department is not always aware that the software is no longer used, but the charge is recurring, so it isn't out of the ordinary. It is common to pay extra months for software.

4. Employee Insurance

We all know that health insurance costs have been rising faster than inflation for at least a decade or more. In most cases, employers have had to cut insurance benefits and push more burden onto the employees. There are many ways to shop for insurance. Of course, you can use a broker who shops the common carriers each year. You could join a PEO (Professional Employer Organization) which will pool all employees, manage payroll and HR, and save on Workers Compensation. This is a great solution for employers with 5-100 employees.

5. Interest Expense / Income

Treasury and Debt Management should be reviewed regularly. Some businesses get stuck in hard money lending or factoring at 15-20%. There are many different banks that can offer different solutions to help lower your interest rate. I am not a fan of much debt. If you have it or need a line of credit, it is important to get the best rate you can.

Don't overlook interest income. With one client of mine that was stockpiling cash and wanted a low-risk solution, we increased the interest income rate by about 0.75% which will produce $30,000-$40,000 in additional interest income over the next 3 years.

An Interesting Scenario

We all know that saving money will increase profits. We get busy, time passes, and everything gets more expensive. A regular review of expenses can be quite profitable. Consider the following small business scenario:

- This $3 million business grows on average by 10% each year for 20 years.

- The company reviews expenses yearly to save on average 1% each year.

- They reinvest the savings back into the business which is an average of an 8% cost of capital.

- Over 20 years, the business will have total profits during this time of an additional $3.1 million.

I am sure anyone would like those results, and with some intentional effort each year, it is very possible.

Figure 10.1: Expense Savings Impact over 20 Years

Year	Revenue	Expense Savings	Future Value
1	$ 3,000,000	$ 30,000	$129,471
2	$ 3,300,000	$ 33,000	$131,869
3	$ 3,630,000	$ 36,300	$134,311
4	$ 3,993,000	$ 39,930	$136,798
5	$ 4,392,300	$ 43,923	$139,331
6	$ 4,831,530	$ 48,315	$141,911
7	$ 5,314,683	$ 53,147	$144,539
8	$ 5,846,151	$ 58,462	$147,216
9	$ 6,430,766	$ 64,308	$149,942
10	$ 7,073,843	$ 70,738	$152,719
11	$ 7,781,227	$ 77,812	$155,547
12	$ 8,559,350	$ 85,594	$158,428
13	$ 9,415,285	$ 94,153	$161,361
14	$ 10,356,814	$ 103,568	$164,350
15	$ 11,392,495	$ 113,925	$167,393
16	$ 12,531,745	$ 125,317	$170,493
17	$ 13,784,919	$ 137,849	$173,650
18	$ 15,163,411	$ 151,634	$176,866
19	$ 16,679,752	$ 166,798	$180,141
20	$ 18,347,727	$ 183,477	$183,477
Total	$ 171,824,998	$ 1,718,250	$ 3,099,814

Call to Clarity

Review your expenses and find an area where you should look to save. Most likely one of the above categories is worth taking a second look.

CHAPTER 11

WHERE IS THE CASH GOING?

Once, I attended a conference which I thoroughly enjoyed and was motivated by the caliber of people and the content. At the end of the first day, the leader presented an option to get extra coaching and accountability. I had been struggling to accomplish a couple of key goals the previous year and desperately wanted the coaching.

After a very convincing presentation on the value of investing in yourself, they passed out packets with a card to sign up. It was a one-time fee of $10,000 or 8 payments of $1,500 plus a $750 nonrefundable fee. Therefore, it would cost $10,000 if I had the cash now or $12,750 over the next 8 months. Of course, as a finance guy, I calculated the effective interest of making payments to be over 40%. Ouch. The problem is that I didn't have the $10,000 to pay for the workshop. What do I do? The workshops were filling up and I knew I needed the help. It was so tempting, but ultimately decided that if I didn't have the cash for the one-time fee, then I should not do it.

There is an interesting challenge between profitability and cash flow. Businesses tend to run daily on cash flow, but we need to make longer term decisions based on profitability. In this case, I needed to step back and understand the true cost. I am very motivated now to save the cash so I can take advantage of great opportunities in the future, but not at the risk of paying over 40% more.

Four Common Cash Problems

Do you find yourself managing your business by looking at your bank account? When cash gets low, do you get nervous and start cutting everything? Do you go through your contacts and emails to find lost billings? Do you start calling clients for past due payments? Does low cash ruin your weekend?

Now, on the other hand, you could be complacent when you *have* enough cash. There are many reasons for a high or low cash balance in the bank, which makes managing your business based on your bank cash balance a dangerous way to operate.

Why is this dangerous? I will give you a few examples.

Cash Problem #1

Your profit is really good for the year, and you are excited about the future of your business. The problem is that you seem to have much less cash than the Income Statement in your accounting system indicates. But, your profit is high, so you continue to spend and hire. You have to borrow more from your line of credit to survive.

Where is Your Cash #1

Most likely there is something happening on the Balance Sheet. The first place to look is distributions. Many owners will take distributions which aren't typically reported on the Income Statement. You have to account for your draws from this business. Another area might be Property & Equipment. Generally Accepted Accounting Principles (GAAP) reports this on your

Balance Sheet. Other areas might be Inventory and Accounts Receivable.

Cash Problem #2

You had the best year ever for your business. You decide to use your extra cash to pay yourself more in distributions and buy additional equipment. Your tax CPA says you owe more tax than ever and are in the highest tax bracket, but you didn't set aside this cash. Now, you have to take on debt to pay your tax bill.

Where is Your Cash #2

Paying more in taxes typically does mean you had a good year, but you have to set this money aside. Consider setting aside up to 30-40% of your operating profit for tax in a separate bank account.

Cash Problem #3

You billed your new client in advance for future work. You purchased equipment and materials for the project and hired contract labor. The project went longer than expected and you paid more for labor than estimated. You used some of this money to pay for operating expenses to keep your business going. Suddenly you need to purchase a major item for the project, but you don't have the cash to do so. You have to borrow money to complete the project and provide the service you told the client you would deliver.

Where is Your Cash #3

Billing in advance is a great idea but it can make your cash balance look better than it really is. You could set up a separate bank account for these types of expenses. At least make sure the cash for materials, labor, and product for this project is set aside. Using a separate bank account is an easy way to see where you are. Understand your true cost and markup the project accordingly. Include padding for any potential cost overruns.

Cash Problem #4

You have been so busy that you have not been consistently billing your clients. Therefore, you go back for the last three months and bill your clients but find that some of them are not paying because it has been too long. You don't have time to call and collect old invoices. Months go by and now it has been over six months since you have provided the work. You don't have any leverage and feel you have to either write it off, send it to collections, or maybe go to small claims court. Who has time for that?

Where is Your Cash #4

One of the easiest ways to prevent most of this is consistent billing and collections. Bill your customers on a regular basis and they will be more likely to approve the invoice. Also, it is easier to collect smaller amounts. Collections are easier when you follow up consistently. Who gets paid first? It will most likely be the business that contacts their clients on a consistent basis.

Cash Profit

You did not go into business to lose money. You want to be profitable and grow. It is important to put some of this money back into your business, but there is nothing wrong with taking distributions. In the book *Profit First*, Mike Michalowicz suggests taking all revenue and putting a percentage into a profit account at another bank entirely. You need to have profits to help you grow and be sustainable.

Cash balances can be misleading, so separating bank accounts between profit, tax, operating expenses, payroll, and revenue can be helpful.

Five Reasons Debt is the New Slavery

The rich rules over the poor; and the borrower becomes the lender's slave. Proverbs 22:7

Nearly 10 years ago, my wife and I had over $50,000 (not including the mortgage) in debt ranging from credit cards, student loans, and an auto loan. Together we went through the book *Total Money Makeover* by Dave Ramsey. Over the next two years, we paid off this debt with an income of about $100k per year. It took intentional focus and sacrifices that were not popular or easy. Ramsey recommends eventually building up a six-month emergency fund, which we accomplished shortly after. We felt so much more at peace once the debt was gone and we had an emergency fund. In 2015, I lost my job and I had to suddenly explore new opportunities with four kids and a wife who home-schools them. I was very thankful for the emergency fund.

As mentioned earlier, I decided to start my own business providing accounting and finance services (fractional CFO services) to small businesses and non-profits. There is no way we could have done this without the emergency fund. The only debt bill was our mortgage, so we were able to last much longer building up the business.

For those who are business owners, whether full-time or on the side, there is also a significant temptation to get into debt. I don't think this is necessary most of the time.

As a business owner, debt can be quite burdensome and requires a ton of work. Below are five reasons why I would avoid debt as much as possible.

1. Distracting and Time-Consuming

There are plenty of distractions that keep us from strategically working on our business. I won't go through them all, but you don't need another stress to worry about. Lenders will ask you to review the debt and send them reports. You might have to apply for new debt, and the application process is time-consuming. Also, you have to make more payments and keep records. Not only do you have more emails, bills, and administrative work, but you are losing valuable time. Whenever you are spending time on tasks related to dealing with debt, you are not spending time on business development, servicing your customers, or focusing on strategies to grow and add more value in less time.

2. Forces Bad Decisions

How could debt force you to make a bad decision? You could decide to accept a client that is not ideal because you desperately need the business to pay the debt. You might decide to work harder and longer to pay off debt at the risk of personal health and time with kids and family. Sometimes even hitting a certain ratio that the bank requires may not be ideal for your business plan.

3. False Sense of Security

What if you are in the habit of looking at your bank account to decide how well your business is doing? When you see a lot of cash in the bank, you spend more and expand. According to the book *Profit First*, this is a common habit among business owners. If you received cash due to a loan, it is not a reason to go on a spending spree. You might feel better and more secure, but your Net Worth has dropped.

4. Too Much Growth Too Fast

It is tempting to grow faster than you can handle when you have the cash to spend, hire, and expand at quick levels. The problem is that with each level, you experience new devils. We should always be growing, but we also need time to develop the processes, training, and strategies to grow smart. Otherwise, you can create chaos. You could create a stressful place to work with high employee turnover and low profit margins. In fact, you may even be losing money, but you are growing too fast to notice it.

5. Loss of Control

What if you had a bank call your loan? This could ruin your business. Anytime you are relying on a lender to keep your business afloat, you have lost control. The stress of this is overwhelming and can have a negative impact on your enjoyment of being a business owner.

Hopefully you can see how debt adds to distraction, stress, bad decisions, and loss of control. I can't imagine that anyone would want to work for or create a business like this. Therefore, even though it is hard, we should work to avoid debt. It is amazing how when we work within certain constraints we can figure out how to do something. I am not saying it is easy, but it is more rewarding and more peaceful. Also, it makes finance much more fun.

Call to Clarity

Do you struggle with cash flow? What is the top area of concern from those mentioned in this chapter? If still uncertain, review your Balance Sheet or contact a good financial consultant or fractional CFO who can help.

PART 3

HOW DO YOU REACH YOUR DESTINATION FASTER?

We have discussed in Part 1 about understanding where you are today with your financial mindset. Once you have the correct mindset, you will better value how solid financials will lead you toward your dreams. Then, in Part 2, we discussed your financial destination through revenue forecasting, expense management, and controlling cash flow.

Now in Part 3 we will discuss how you can get to your destination faster. We will dive deeper into discipline, focus, and consistency to keep you on track. We will look at productivity hacks and how focused goals can keep us from getting distracted and off course. We all will spend our lives working to improve these areas. We all have our strengths which need to be enhanced to help us on this journey.

Let's start with discipline. It is not a scary as you think.

CHAPTER 12

HOW TO STAY DISCIPLINED AND FOCUSED

I had a week that started in a funk. I found out that I didn't get a client I had worked many hours trying to close. Also, I was stuck doing client work that I found quite unexciting. Yes, I know this is part of life, so I don't want to complain. The challenge is that with my personality, sometimes this mindset can completely sabotage me. If a funk like this lasts several days, then I can lose weeks or maybe months toward my long-term goal.

What gets you in a funk when it comes to your business? Do you ever find yourself wanting to give up and start over? Maybe you feel you need a vacation. That may be the case, but do you feel this way often? Do you wonder why you even started this business and start thinking about ways to get out of it? I had to make a list of why I started my business, and I review it sometimes. Maybe you feel like there is nobody to talk to. Your spouse may not really understand. Your friends might not be business owners, so they can't be helpful in this area. Are you afraid other people might discourage you more? What can you do?

I must say there is only one good answer, and it might seem boring – discipline.

Discipline is the act of continually doing what you know you should do even when you don't want to.

This discipline is necessary for personal development, study, exercise, writing a book, being creative, business development, meetings, launching a business and so much more. We have to do it. How do we tell the difference between discipline and stupidity or insanity? You may have heard that insanity is doing the same things over and over and expecting different results. We might have to adjust, but overall, we need discipline because we can't adjust all the time. We need to stick it out for a while. How long do we stick it out? Thirty days, three months, a year?

Below are 10 ideas that can help you stay disciplined in the midst of a tough week, or month, for that matter.

1. Reach out to three people to encourage them (e-mail and text are fine). It takes less time than you think. Encouragement just makes you feel better. I think there is nothing wrong with making another person feel good so that it makes you feel good in return.

2. Try exercising daily. Even five minutes of pushups, sit-ups, or burpees can be helpful. This physical discipline affects other areas of your life.

3. Write down three things you are grateful for. It is hard to stay depressed or discouraged and be grateful at the same time.

4. Read your "Why" list. If you don't have a list, I would encourage you to write down the reasons why you are working toward a goal or dream.

5. Pray for strength and energy and reach out to others for prayer. Even if they don't understand, it might be good to have someone who can listen.

6. Write down your thoughts. Blogging and journaling help me.

7. Go for a walk, enjoy God's creation, and play.

8. Stay on track doing what you set out to do for at least 30 days. If you still hate what you are doing, look to adjust. Is it a project or a client?

9. Consider how much of your time you are doing something you are proficient in and passionate about. We should strive to continually do more that inspires us so that we can produce our best work for others.

10. Do the hard things early in the day because studies show that willpower decreases throughout the day.

Discipline is the bridge between goals and accomplishment. Jim Rohn

It was character that got us out of bed, commitment that moved us to action, and discipline that enabled us to follow through. Zig Ziglar

The day always comes when we want to give up. We wonder why we embarked on the journey we are on. Think about what would happen if we quit. What are the consequences of losing momentum and starting over later? How does this affect your family, employees, followers, and platform? I speak to myself as much as to you.

Don't Let the Word "Discipline" Scare You

The word "discipline" makes me think of waking up early to run 10 miles and eating cucumbers and lettuce all day. It sounds like no fun and a lot of work that very few people could stick with. I also think of the military. I was not in the military, but from what I have heard or seen on TV, it sounds extremely difficult with no freedom. As a kid, I was disciplined on a regular basis from my dad, and that was certainly not fun at all.

So, what kind of discipline am I talking about?

In the book *The 10x Rule*, Grant Cardone defines discipline as an orderly, prescribed conduct that will get you what you want. He says, "Discipline is what you use to complete any activity until the activity – regardless of how uncomfortable – becomes your normal operating procedure."

In the *The Mastery Journal*, John Lee Dumas defines discipline as "being able to stay on task and still make progress even when you're feeling unmotivated, distracted, or discouraged."

So how does discipline help Finance and Accounting? Below are five ways.

1. Discipline Saves You Time

The best way that discipline saves time is through consistent financial reporting. If your accounting and financial reports are updated monthly, it will be easier to update and take less time than if you let them build over months or even years. Yes, I have seen this a few times. Cleaning up months or years of accounting and financial reports is always much more difficult and time-consuming than if you do this as you go.

There was a house down the street with a sign that said, "Coming Soon." The sign had been there for months. The yard was a disaster and kept getting worse. What if they didn't mow the yard all summer? You couldn't use just any lawn mower to handle it. You would need special equipment. The neighbors were complaining about snakes and other critters, so it could be dangerous. I am sure after mowing, everything would look dead. What if you never maintained your financials? What would happen? Not only would you not know how you are doing as a business, it would be quite challenging and expensive to clean up.

2. Discipline Gives You Better Information

If you update your revenue, expenses, and Balance Sheet on a monthly basis, you can use this information to make better financial decisions. Consistent financials are great for trending and forecasting your cash flow. If you want to hire employees, buy equipment, or need financing, it is helpful to see your cash flow trends. It is significantly easier to make these decisions with consistent trends and financial reporting by month.

Michael Hyatt and Daniel Harkavy's book *Living Forward* gives a great analogy that makes a lot of sense. Many of us have planned a vacation before. The first thing we do when planning a vacation is to decide where we want to go. This will help us determine other variables such as clothing, transportation, and activities to do when we get there.

3. Discipline is Proactive

If you have discipline, you are in control of your calendar instead of waiting for someone to tell you what to do. Have you been on email all day before and didn't get anything done that you set out to do that day? Email is a great example of being reactive in many cases. It is a necessary evil for communication but can derail your day. Be proactive and use the best part of your day to focus on the tasks you need to accomplish to meet your goals for your business. My time is in the morning. I have found that if I don't start my day being disciplined, then the rest of the day tends to be highly unproductive.

4. Discipline is Essential for Revenue Growth

Business development requires a consistent approach to networking, reaching out to people, and following up. Some people do business development all the time, and others are performing a hybrid of business development, business strategy, management, client services, and operational work. This depends mainly on the size of the company as to how many roles you fill. Any business owner needs to have a disciplined, repetitive approach to business development. You should not let up on this so that the momentum grows your business. This takes discipline because there may be days you don't feel like doing business development. Client or employee issues might take over and you will think you don't have time for business development.

Developing business helps in many areas. There are unintended benefits that could help your existing clients. I find that by networking, I have better ideas to help my business grow at new levels. Who wants to sit around answering emails all day anyway?

5. Discipline Sets the Example for Others

> *If your actions inspire others to dream more, learn more, do more, and become more, you are a leader.* John Quincy Adams

People want to follow successful people, and the most successful people I know are disciplined. We all need to have employees, contractors, consultants, and colleagues following our lead of accomplishing more and making a larger impact.

Summary

Discipline provides many other benefits, so why does it scare us? Is it because we get disappointed when we get off track?

Is it because other people seem to be having more fun with their undisciplined lifestyle?

Do you want to save time? Do you want better financial information? Would you rather have control of your time, or do you want someone else to be in charge of your time? Don't we all desire more revenue growth? Don't we want to be a good example for our employees, contractors, or even friends and family? If so, then we need discipline. Let's all embrace it. We might mess up, but move on and get back on the discipline track to success.

Call to Clarity

Take one of the discipline habits as mentioned in this chapter and put it on the schedule. Practice this discipline regularly, and eventually it will become a new, good habit.

CHAPTER 13

FOCUS ON STRENGTHS

I recommend the StrengthsFinder 2.0 assessment (strengthsfinder.com) in order to learn your strengths and how you can best use them to be successful.

My strengths are Analytical, Discipline, Responsibility, Consistency, and Harmony. Without going into them much, they are not suited well for an impromptu Toastmasters Evaluation Speech contest, except maybe for showing up. I guess showing up is half the battle because I ended up 2nd place in the Area contest by showing up and following through. There is a Strengths Finder coach who is part of my club, and I asked her about this. She said, "Our strengths don't tell us what we DO, but rather they tell us HOW we do things." In other words, by understanding our strengths and maximizing those, we can be excellent in our own way.

So how do we maximize our strengths in order to reach our destination faster? Below are five ways that can help.

1. Understand Yourself

We probably will spend most of our lives doing this. The earlier we understand ourselves and how we function, the more we can lead others. You might have heard that you can't lead others until you lead yourself. One of the first steps is to take the StrengthsFinder 2.0 assessment. There are also many other assessments such as the DiSC Profile or Myers Briggs that are helpful.

I would say that sometimes when I take these assessments, I think of them as limiting. For example, if it says you are an introvert, then you could feel a limiting belief that you cannot lead or influence others as well as an extrovert. We should be careful not to take the negative stance, but the positive aspect of the strengths.

2. Understand the "Sharpen the Saw" Concept

In Steven Covey's famous book *7 Habits of Highly Effective People*, he has a story of two people chopping down a tree in the woods. One person is sawing as fast and hard as he can. He is working extremely hard. The other person is taking a break periodically and doesn't appear to be working nearly as hard. Eventually, the tree of the person who was taking periodic breaks came down first. This made the first person upset. He asked the other person how his tree came down first when he stopped for so many breaks. He simply said that each time he sat down to take a break, he would sharpen the saw.

We all must work toward improvement so that we become better versions of ourselves. Once you know your strengths, then work to understand how you can use those strengths. It is easy to get frustrated, depressed, or disappointed. Your goal is simply to try to be a better version of who you were yesterday. The comparison trap can be counterproductive.

3. Listen to Podcasts and Other Leaders

I can't begin to tell you how much I have learned from Podcasts or listening to the wisdom of other leaders. It is essential for anyone to be successful. Have you ever been listening to the radio and a song comes on that you have heard 20 times in the last week? Then, it rolls to a 10-minute commercial break. You then try other stations, but it seems that they all timed their commercial breaks at the same time. Then, you start to listen to talk radio only to discover that you start to get depressed as you think the nation might break into civil war or a racial riot. Depending on your nature, this could have very negative effects on your performance. My suggestion is to listen to quality podcasts.

4. Read More

One thing about reading is that there is no lack of information for us to consume. There are probably more people than ever wanting our attention, and it is easy to just tune it all out. Now with Audible it is easier than ever to read books. The only thing about Audible is that many of us only retain 20% of what we hear, so we probably forget to apply the concepts. I recommend E-books so you can highlight and then go back and review and download your highlights. Also, throw in a fiction book from time to time to help you grow more.

5. Use Technology

As you know, technology is changing at a rapid pace all the time. Sometimes it can lead to more distractions, such as misuse of smartphones. Overall, it can help us do routine and boring tasks much faster; then, we have more time to sharpen our skills. I am finding new technology all the time, so it can be distracting just trying something new. Consider technology that helps you process emails, remember tasks, organize information, or learn something in a flexible and inexpensive way.

As I think more about the speech contest, I am glad I did it. At first, I thought it might have been a waste of time. I ended up using it as a blog post. I learned more about myself and how I can use my strengths better. I even ended up sharing contact information with the other contestant when I realized there could be business opportunities. Not a bad way to sharpen my strengths.

Call to Clarity

Take the Strengths Finder 2.0 assessment to know your strengths. If you have already done this, review it and write down one area where you can maximize one of your strengths.

CHAPTER 14

WHY CONSISTENCY IS POWERFUL

In order to truly maximize our strengths, we need a consistent approach to build the habits that will help us. What do you think about these questions?

Is it better to exercise for 10 minutes every day or 30 minutes a day 3 times a week?

Is it better to have an hour to read a chapter in a book or read a little bit when you have a chance?

If you have a project to do, is it better to do a little each day or in large chunks of time?

These are questions that came to mind when I read *The Slight Edge* by Jeff Olson. There is a battle between doing something a little at a time versus focusing in larger time chunks. As a general rule, focused attention in larger time periods is preferable. But we live in the real world of distractions and chaos at work and home. With our smartphones and busy schedules, it can be hard to set aside a two-hour block to focus. It can be hard to find 30 minutes or more to exercise.

What is the alternative? Do we not exercise until we have enough time? Do we not read, pray, meditate, or even start a task until we have enough time to do it well? I feel like there is a tendency to say to ourselves, "I have 10 minutes, which is not enough time to do much, so I will check email or Facebook." I know I have had this thought many times.

Here are five reasons why consistency beats quality.

1. Good Habits are Formed by a Consistent Daily Routine

If you do something every day, it will become so ingrained in your daily routine that it will come to define who you are. If you decide to exercise in the morning, even for 10 minutes, you will miss not doing it. Something will not seem right, but suppose you miss one 10-minute exercise session a week. You have still managed to work out six days out of the week. On the other hand, suppose you have set a goal to work out one hour per day for three days a week. If something comes up that keeps you from getting your full hour in, you may not exercise. Missing one time a week on this three-day schedule suddenly brings you down to two times a week. Now you are probably more discouraged, and you may not see the point in exercising at all. In this case, the focus on quality did you no favors. True consistency has been gained with the 10- minute, everyday approach.

2. Daily Activity Equals Increased Productivity

Anything done daily tends to increase productivity because you start to operate more on auto pilot. If you drive to work or to a client on a regular basis, do you remember every turn? Your brain doesn't have to think as much because the habit is ingrained in you.

Some things are better to do weekly or monthly, such as certain financial activities. There will still be increased productivity because consistency is built up by doing the activity at the same time each week or month. We tend to easily remember what we did the same time last week or month.

3. Mastering the Mundane Leads to Success

There is a whole chapter devoted to mastering the mundane in *The Slight Edge*. Financial success is usually a consistent practice of spending less than you make and investing a little of what you save. Saving 10% of what you make from age 25 to 65 at an average income of $70,000 per year at a 10% return will leave you about $3.1 million for your golden years. That is saving $8,000 a year, $580 a month or $20 a day. Some of us spend $20 a day on Starbucks and lunch. In the book *The Millionaire Next Door*, the authors give examples of people who did little things each day, each week, and each month to become millionaires and you wouldn't even know it.

4. More Peace (Less Stress)

Doing a little each day makes you feel as if you are accomplishing your goals. On the other hand, if you wait until you have more time, you will feel guilty and possibly more stressed as procrastination, delays, or other unforeseen events keep you from doing what you know you need to do.

Recently, I desired to build a habit to read from a good book each day. If I only have 15 minutes, I feel better because I know I did something rather than having the thought of not doing it on my mind all day.

5. Big Projects are Not so Big

We know that it is easier to break big projects down into small chunks or sprints. Have you heard about eating an elephant one bite at a time?

Cleaning up a business' financials or hitting a revenue goal seems challenging. Maybe you want to grow your business by 20% and that is $500,000 more revenue. That may seem like a lot, but it is more manageable if you say that it is $42,000 a month or about $10,000 a week. By breaking it down this way, you can better assess the resources needed and make necessary adjustments along the way.

In summary, I argue that consistency is better than quality. Don't let the idea of doing something perfect or with the highest quality paralyze you. Good habits performed daily, weekly, or even monthly lead to more productivity. Master the mundane and live more in peace. Finally, big projects will begin to seem manageable. Consistency leads to success while quality and perfection can lead to frustration. Consistency might not be perfect, but it can lead to more perfection in due time.

• • •

A ceramics teacher decided to split his class into two groups. One group was focused solely on the quantity of the work they produced, and the other was focused on quality. When it came to grading time, he noticed that the works of highest quality were all produced by the group being graded for quantity. The "quantity" group had learned from their mistakes and improved each time. The quality group only had theories and little to show for their work. (Bayles, 1993)

You might ask what this story has to do with finance and accounting for business. There are many interpretations of this story that you can find online, but I am going to focus on consistency. I think that businesses improve when they have consistent reporting, metrics, and processes. Below are five reasons consistency is important in your business finances.

1. Momentum

Lou Holtz said, "In this world, you're either growing or you're dying so get in motion and grow." I heard this from a small business owner and it got me thinking about momentum. Suppose you have a consistent process to reach out to a certain number of people a day and keep track of it. This consistent practice will build momentum, and over time, produce results.

In business, monthly financial reports, a forecast model, and the current budget should be reviewed regularly and compared to last month and last year's financial results. This review can provide the momentum needed to help you reach your financial goals.

2. Trending and Analysis

In financial planning and analysis, trending is an important tool to forecast future months. It is common for me to go into a business and notice that revenue and expenses are not matching by month. I don't want to get heavy on accounting, but one principle to keep in mind is that revenue and expenses must match the period that they are recorded on the Income Statement.

For example, in the media/marketing industry it is common to have pass through costs that are billed to clients and paid back out to other vendors. If a client pre-bills and records all the revenue in one month, but the passthrough costs are recorded in another, it is challenging to determine the revenue. For one thing, the revenue is not recorded correctly, but also the revenue will fluctuate each month simply because of the timing of the processing.

Consistency in accounting and reporting is essential each month so we can truly see how the business is performing and trend the revenue into future months.

3. Communication

Once certain reports and metrics are established, then consistency improves communication. It is essential that each month a business reviews the Income Statement, Balance Sheet, Statement of Cash Flow, and other Key Performance Indicators (KPIs).

Once everyone has been trained on how to review the key financial reports, the presentation, delivery, and commentary should be consistent so executives can quickly understand what is going on and adjust if necessary.

4. Process

The most efficient process in any organization is one that has been fine-tuned and is repeated the same way each time. A consistent process decreases errors and can be quickly performed over and over without much thought. I am a firm believer in continually improving processes. Just as in the example of the ceramic pots, when a process is completed over and over, it is perfected and tweaked over time.

Develop a consistent month-end accounting and reporting process so that it can be performed more quickly, automated if possible, and become less error prone.

5. Bankers, Auditors, and Investors

One thing I know from generating and reviewing financial statements for 20 years is that bankers, auditors, and investors do not like surprises. They want the financials to consistently grow, and revenue, expenses, and margin to improve in a systematic way. Anytime revenue drops unexpectedly, or there is a big expense in a certain month, it will have to be analyzed and explained.

Consistency is essential if you want to keep investors, the bank, or even auditors happy. They are trained to look for anomalies and any red flags.

In summary, consistency is vital for your business and financial reporting because it builds momentum, ensures more accurate trending and analysis, and results in more effective and timely communication across the company. Also, consistency will ensure a quality process and keep the bank, auditors, and investors happy.

I know for some of you it may seem like a long way before you have consistency. Maybe you are in a chaotic environment due to growth and inconsistency. Just like with the ceramics story, focus on quantity instead of quality. Start doing something today to improve your business reporting and analysis, and you will get better with time. With each passing month, this consistent activity will deliver unexpected results and the chaos will decrease.

Call to Clarity

What is one consistent business activity that you want to start to implement? It could be a consistent accounting, marketing, business development activity or maybe something more related to personal health.

CHAPTER 15

WHAT CAN WE DO TO ADD VALUE?

Have you ever been stuck getting tasks done that don't seem to add value? Do you feel like you spend all your time merely doing what you are supposed to do each day or week and no time to look for ways to add value? What do I mean by adding value? In a business or even a nonprofit setting, it usually comes in one of three ways:

Money: We add value by finding ways to increase revenue or decrease expenses.

Time: We add value by finding ways to save time.

Impact: We add value by increasing excitement, influence, or hope with customers, employees, or even society in general.

Have you been in a situation such as an employee review, a client meeting, or a board meeting and had to explain what you have accomplished? No one is going to say I answered 1,000 emails or I took care of routine and everyday activities. Yes, routine activities are necessary. These activities are essential or everything good falls apart. We have to clean our house, or it will become unsanitary and hard to find any-thing. Also, we need to maintain the accounting, pay the bills, and collect unpaid invoices or we won't be in business long.

However, if you spend all your time on these routine activities, you are not setting yourself apart from the competition nor improving your business to stay up with technology, stay efficient, or stay relevant. So, what can we do to add value to our organizations? How can we do this? Here are some ideas that have been helping me.

1. **Wake up Early.** Each morning should consist of prayer, reading, exercise, journaling, and affirmations. A great book on this subject is called *The Miracle Morning* by Hal Elrod.

2. **Listen.** I have had a quiet time most mornings for years, but what I have started doing recently is lis-tening. I have started listening to God. I know this might seem weird to some people, but I believe as a Christian that God wants to speak to us. We just have to listen. I recommend reading *2 Chairs – The Secret That Changes Everything*. The premise of the book is that God who created everything knows the future and knows us better than we know ourselves. He wants a relationship with us, but we have to listen to Him. We aren't telling Him anything He doesn't know, but He does have a lot to share with us. Why not take the chance and try it?

3. **Ask.** I recommend asking clients, employees, super-visors, or even spouses or children how to add value. You might phrase it differently, though. Maybe ask them in one of the following ways:

   • How can I make your life easier?

   • How can I save you time?

- What is something you would like to change about me or my business?

4. **Create a Value Matrix.** Write down one thing you are going to do to add value each month or at least every three months. Do this for all of your important relationships. Since I provide fractional CFO services for clients, I created a value matrix with my clients listed in columns and months in rows. See an example below.

Figure 15.1: Value Matrix

Value Matrix			Client 1
Jan 20XX		Time	Saved 10 hours due to new system
		Money	Saved $10,000 in cedit card fees
		Impact	
Feb 20XX		Time	
		Money	Lowered Health Insurance costs by $10,000 annually
		Impact	Increased email list by 20%

5. **Plan your week and day**. Plan what you are going to do each day on your calendar the night before. Also, plan each week ahead of time. Be sure to schedule time to work on value-adding activities. Don't get lost in being reactive to answering emails and issues that arise. Purchase *The Freedom Journal* by John Lee Dumas or the *Full Focus Planner* by Michael Hyatt & Co. to help with this planning. These are great resources to help meet any goal.

Becoming Valuable to Add Value

Have you been doing the same processes for years and don't know why? Are you afraid to change something because you think it will break? Do you subscribe to the mindset, "If it ain't broke, don't fix it?" The problem with that philosophy is that this fast-moving world will pass you by. The horse and buggy were not broken when the automobile came. Or more recently, we thought the old flip phones and even Blackberries were great until the iPhone.

Technology is changing at a rapid pace. Corporate employment is not the safe job it used to be. I heard someone say that in 20 years, 50% of all jobs will be entrepreneurs and contractors. Is that possible?

I once thought accounting was a safe profession. There would always be the need for accountants. However, at one of my corporate jobs, most of the accounting was getting outsourced to countries such as India at a fraction of the cost.

We should always assess our processes, our skills, and the latest technology. My job as a CFO for small businesses is to stay on top of the latest trends and to be strategic. We should all strive to add value regularly. Here are five ways to add value to any organization.

1. Consistently Read the Best Books

Twice this week I was reminded of the importance of reading good books. The first was an article by Daniel Ally called "5 Tips to Read 100 Books a Year." He mentions learning how to speed read and not read a book cover to cover. I must admit that this strategy might be difficult at first, but most books don't have a lot of new concepts. Most likely there are a few nuggets to apply to your life, and you want to get to the point as fast as possible.

In the book *The Slight Edge*, Jeff Olson mentions consistently reading 10 pages from a good life-changing book every day. It seems easy to do 10 pages. Think of how much you would read in one year. Consistently learning a little bit each day will not look like much after one day or even a week. But after a year of reading over 3,600 pages of high-quality material, you will see a difference.

2. Stop Doing Busy Work

My company was hired to perform all accounting and finance which included transactional bookkeeping as well as strategic CFO work. During the first week, I found myself spending all my time receiving payments, entering bills, and cutting checks. I knew I should not be spending all my time doing this. My value is elsewhere. Therefore, I hired a couple of bookkeepers to help me.

We need to look at all of our processes and decide if we should cut some of them or delegate. What if a process seems redundant or unnecessary? Should we keep doing it? What if we stop and it causes a problem? If a redundant or useless process needs to go away, we should consider the risk and reward. We save time by stopping a task at the risk of possibly needing information we no longer have. I would argue to be fast at cutting redundant processes, so you quickly understand the effect.

3. Spend More Time Thinking and Less Time Doing

Thinking today seems like a lost art. We spend quite a bit of our free time watching Netflix or checking Facebook or sports. Sometimes, there is no time to think. What if we kept asking ourselves why we are doing this task? One night my wife and I spent 15 minutes trying to find something to watch on Netflix. We said it was movie night, so we were going to watch something even if it was horrible and our brains turned to mush. We had done this many times before. We couldn't find anything good, so we turned off the TV and went to bed early. Great decision. Why hadn't we done this before?

4. Test New Technology

Technology changes all the time, so get in the habit of testing new software. There is no reason to keep using the old technology/processes just because you are afraid a new one won't work. For a small business, the worst that can happen is that you are back to the old paper-driven processes. Most likely, you can make it work in the long run.

5. Be Intentional

This last point is almost a repeat of the first four points. In order to be successful, whether you are a business owner or not, make a conscious effort to think about everything you are doing. Is this a waste of time? Does this have value? Is there a better way?

My suggestion is to schedule time on your calendar to read, to study new technologies, and to think. Get rid of what you shouldn't be doing and delegate what others can do better, cheaper, and more passionately.

Stop wasting time and start doing what you love in a more efficient and profitable way and with more excitement.

Call to Clarity

Pick one thing that you want to start doing that will help you add value to your clients, customers, employees, etc.

CHAPTER 16

THE KEYS TO PRODUCTIVE IMPROVEMENTS

Recently, as an entrepreneur, I was discouraged by another business owner. I was complaining about my workload and the hours I was spending. He told me to get used to it because I would be working a lot of hours for the first few years. With four kids and a marriage that is important to me, I found this to be a depressing thought. I like working, but within reason. It isn't healthy to work too many hours and not have time to rejuvenate and nurture relationships. So, what do business owners do?

AUTOMATION

What do I mean by automation? This sounds like robotics or some kind of industrial tooling mechanism that would not be applicable. In an online course from Michael Hyatt, he broke down automation into routines, templates, processes, and technology. Here are four ways automation can be used financially in your business.

1. Financial Routines

Depending on the size of the business, there are weekly, monthly, quarterly, and annual routines to ensure success for your business. Can you imagine if you forgot to comb your hair and brush your teeth in your morning routine? All day you would look like you had just gotten out of bed and you would probably have bad breath. Your business is the same. It is important to reconcile your Balance Sheet and review your Income Statement on a regular basis.

2. Standard Processes

We all have processes in what we do. I know some people don't like processes, and I realize that "process" sounds very formal. We all have a process in our head, but to communicate to our team, we should write it down and train others. You need sales and revenue processes for business development. Then, you need contracts, billing, and collections processes for getting cash. It is important to have a payables process to pay for materials, operating expenses, and to pay employees. Also, you need cash management processes for saving for taxes, abnormal expenses, bonuses, distributions, and profits.

3. Templates

If you find that you are emailing or answering the same question repeatedly, you need a template. You can use email signatures to create common emails with attachments. Also, Google Gmail has a "Canned Response" feature. A Finance Manager at one of my clients found this helpful when sending out monthly reports. Templates are helpful for Expense Reports, Standard Reports, Time Sheets, Contracts, Billing

Reports, etc. There is so much potential here that it has my brain churning.

4. Email Freedom

I have started to dislike email. For some reason, I find myself continually checking it and getting distracted. I think we tend to check email to keep from working on the hard stuff. It is easier to be reactive than proactive. We feel like we are needed, and we like the dopamine hit. The problem is that after spending 2-3 hours stuck in my email, I still have to get all the real work done. There is a tool called Sane Box that is helpful in saving time. It will put emails in folders like Sane News, Sane Bulk, and Sane Later to keep your inbox clean for what is most important. I like the Sane Tomorrow folder. I can put a less urgent email in this folder and the email will be sent to me again tomorrow. Also, using a project management tool like Asana or Slack will keep your conversations and tasks out of email.

Automation is essential to avoid chaos, confusion, and working too many hours. I know we will be working on this regularly as long as we are in business. As a business grows, there will be new challenges. By implementing routines, processes, templates, and technology you will be on your way to more excitement and freedom in your business.

DELEGATION & EMPOWERMENT

Statisticbrain.com states that 25% of all start-ups fail within one year, and 50% of businesses fail within 5 years. This site goes on to explain that "incompetence" is the number one reason for business failure. I know this seems harsh, but it isn't too surprising. It is difficult to be good at everything. Most likely, a business is good at making a product or providing a service, but might not be good at planning, finance, accounting, pricing, taxes, and management.

Let's say you are the 50% that makes it. There is another problem that is common. Many business owners spend too much or all of their time working "in" their business and not "on" their business. An excellent book on this subject is *The E-Myth Revisited* by Michael Gerber. A successful business grows to a point where we need to set up processes, delegate more, and grow to the next level. There is a large difference between being competent in providing the service or product and growing a business and infrastructure with employees, management, accounting, and scalable growth.

As a small business owner or leader of any organization, do you struggle with being involved in every aspect of your growing company? Do you long for the days when it was smaller and you could know everything that was going on? Are you growing so fast and you know you need to hire people, but you worry it will be more work than it is worth? Maybe you are fully aware that you need to delegate, but you simply struggle to let go.

There comes a point in any organization when you must hire and delegate to grow, but it is not as simple as just hiring and all your problems will be solved. You must learn to teach, train, and empower your employees and build processes to ensure the culture stays intact and you trust those you rely on. How do you do that? Phillip Van Hooser defines empowerment as the power to grant your power to someone else. He writes about the "Levels of Empowerment" as listed below:

Level 1: You report; I will decide.

Level 2: Identify the alternatives; suggest one for implementation; I will decide.

Level 3: Report what you intend to do; but wait for my approval.

Level 4: Report what you intend to do; do it unless I say "no."

Level 5: Take action; report what you did.

Level 6: Take action; no further communication is necessary.

How are you working with your team members? What are some problems that can come about due to lack of empowerment or too much empowerment? I have listed certain challenges.

Stuck at Level 1

Once a business owner or leader decides to hire help, the new employee starts out at Level 1 (You report; I will decide) in most cases. You might decide to quickly move to the next level if the person you hired is experienced. Sometimes employees stay at Level 1 too long. Why would someone even consider leaving someone at Level 1?

- Multiple mistakes or errors lead to a lack of trust. In this case, this employee may need to be replaced.

- Leader sometimes lacks confidence to hand over responsibility due to insecurity or fear of losing his job.

- Leader likes control and struggles giving it up.

- Leader lacks time to train employees so they are not ready to go to the next level.

There might be other reasons, but in all the above cases, usually either the employee will leave, or the leader will end up getting frustrated and replace this employee.

Skipping levels

If a business owner or leader needs to relieve responsibility due to being overwhelmed, there is a tendency to move too fast or skip levels altogether.

If an employee goes straight from Level 1 (You report, I decide), to Level 5 (Take action, report what you did), most likely both the manager/owner or employee will get frustrated. The owner will, for a time, feel like everything is good until they find out something was implemented that they don't agree with. The manager will be frustrated because they are stuck with a mess. The employee will be frustrated due to not fully understanding how the manager thinks and makes decisions.

Lack of Communication and Clarity

Lack of clarity is quite common when managers/owners do not take the time to communicate.

As a company grows, communication gets more challenging, so a process needs to be implemented. What are some good ways to communicate with your team? In the book *The Advantage*, Patrick Lencioni states that organizations must have the following 4 disciplines:

- Build a cohesive leadership.

- Create clarity.

- Over-communicate clarity.

- Reinforce clarity.

I'm sure you noticed that he put clarity in there more than once. This proves how important it is to communicate the goals to your team and to make sure everyone knows what needs to be done to be successful and meet those goals.

Inconsistency in Expectations

What if one day a manager expects Level 1 empowerment and another day, Level 3? What if the manager moves the levels depending on workload and mood? It is quite frustrating for the employee to not know what to expect. I am sure this is more common than we want to admit. Inconsistency doesn't work with raising kids, so it sure is not going to work in a business.

It is important to hire and rely on others as you grow your organization. When you do so, empower your employees and communicate on their current level. As they move up to the next level, communicate this also. It is possible that an employee could move back down to Level 1 or 2, but this can get tricky for employee morale. People like to grow and move to the next level. Think of school. Would you like to be stuck in 5th grade or get demoted to 4th grade? Be consistent with your expectations and you will spend less time in chaos and cleaning up messes.

It isn't easy, but we need to be mindful of this because in order to grow our business, team, or leadership skills, we all need to learn the art of empowerment.

In John Maxwell's book *The 21 Irrefutable Laws of Leadership*, he writes about the Law of Empowerment. What is empowerment? Empowerment is giving authority and responsibilities to employees so they can grow, be held accountable, and take ownership. Maxwell states that when secure leaders give power to others, an organization becomes powerful. Great leaders empower others to reach their full potential.

You are probably saying "I can do it faster" or "I can't trust anyone." The first step is to train and begin to give employees more autonomy. Be sure to inspect their work and correct if necessary, but don't give up. Once you have empowered someone to take ownership to do their role well, you (the owner or supervisor) are then free to do other things that are valuable in moving the organization further.

Call to Clarity

Pick one productivity improvement to focus on developing. Is it to get rid of debt, improve automation, or to utilize delegation?

CHAPTER 17

HOW FOCUSED GOALS HELP YOU MOVE FASTER

Early on when I started my CFO Services consulting business, I started a 100-day goal. My number one goal was based on revenue and clients. As most business owners know, revenue cures many problems. I used *The Freedom Journal* by John Lee Dumas to help me meet my goal. Each day for 100 days, I started the morning writing down the following:

1. One thing I am grateful for

2. My 100-day goal

3. My main focus for the day

4. Two things I was doing that day to help me achieve the goal

5. Three things I was going to accomplish that day

6. My action plan for the day – I would make sure everything important was on my calendar.

Before going to bed, I would assess the day by documenting the following:

- Two good things that happened that day
- Two things I struggled with that day
- Two solutions for those struggles
- What is going to make tomorrow a great day?

I learned quite a bit about myself and my process for hitting goals. I will cut to the chase. I did not hit my goal, so don't think that because you adopt the above course of action for 100 days that you will automatically succeed. Even though I didn't hit my goal, I learned from this experience and set a better goal for the next 100 days. So, if it didn't work, then why do this again?

Reason #1 – Repetition Leads to Increased Focus

Whenever we do something over and over again, it becomes a habit. Because I would journal each day all that I mentioned above, I began to feel like something was missing if I didn't do it. It was almost like forgetting to brush my teeth. It became so ingrained in my daily habits that I would more often think about what I am grateful for. Also, during the day, I would often think about my main goal. I began realizing throughout the 100 days how easy it is to get off track. It is easy to allow other people or seemingly good ideas to fill the schedule. I remember driving home from numerous meetings saying to myself, "Now what did that have to do with my main goal?"

Another benefit from repetition is that I began to look at the following day's schedule the night before and to finalize my schedule in the morning. I almost felt like I was not working if I hadn't reviewed my calendar and scheduled my activities.

Reason #2 – Learning from my Mistakes

I definitely made mistakes in those 100 days that kept me from hitting my revenue target. As Albert Einstein said, "Anyone who has never made a mistake has never tried anything new." I learned that I didn't have a good system for keeping track of my meetings and following up with key contacts and referral partners. I have since started using *Vipor* to organize my contacts into different categories (this app calls them Orbits). I make sure that I log meeting notes and put a follow-up task on my calendar right after the first meeting.

Reason #3 – I Most Likely Got Further Than Where I Would Have Been Otherwise

Upon looking back, there are many measurements for hitting a revenue goal. I am doubtful that I would have met and reached out to as many people as I did if I hadn't set this goal. Also, my pipeline of opportunities is larger due to all the work I did to reach the goal.

Reason #4 – Recording and Seeing Progress Breeds Perseverance

It is easy to get frustrated when progress seems slow. I know I have had moments of frustration. There is a tendency for me to focus on the negative. Each day I would be sure to write down the good things that happened. There were some days when I really had to struggle to think of good things. There were other days when it was harder to come up with the struggles (these were few and far between). By writing and getting in the habit of thinking this way, I was able to see progress. *The Freedom Journal* has 10-day sprints and 25-day check-ups. It was fun to see the surprisingly good things that happened in the last 10 or 25 days. The progress helped keep me going.

Reason #5 – Consistency = Success

I am a fan of consistency. I believe consistency helps build habits. So much progress can be made by doing a little bit each day. How did this 100-day plan help with consistency? I started doing important things each day such as reviewing my calendar and scheduling my day. I started keeping track and following up with prospects, strategic partners, and other contacts. The momentum had started so I just needed to keep it going in the next 100 days.

When and How to Make Adjustments to Goals

Before becoming a business owner, I completed a course called "5 Days to Your Best Year Ever" by Michael Hyatt. I focused on writing down goals and making them specific, measurable, actionable, realistic, time-bound, exciting, and relevant. It emphasized reviewing the goals regularly and documenting why we set them in the first place.

I took this course the same year I was laid off. What do we do when something outside our control affects our goals? In the middle of the year, I had another goal, which was to make a significant career change from corporate accounting to personal financial advising. Late in the year, I resigned from that position because I realized I was not utilizing my strengths by spending almost all of my time on high volume selling. What do we do then? Should we stick to goals no matter what? What happens when our goals become out-dated or no longer applicable? What happens when we miss a timeline, or we want to do something different? Life is not as simple as setting a goal, meeting it, and living the life of our dreams. We have challenges, discouragement, distractions, and unforeseen events that make hitting our goals tough.

I have come up with what I believe are the top five reasons why companies and people do not hit their goals. By understanding these reasons, I hope we can improve our odds of succeeding.

1. Fear

I think we should all have at least one stretch goal that pushes us out of our comfort zone. For quite a while, I have had the goals to write a book, create a course, and do a podcast. All of these goals are out of my comfort zone. Also, I am very excited about my CFO Services business and see quite a bit of potential for this in the marketplace, but I still experience some fear and worry about getting new clients and helping them succeed. I heard a pastor at a church say whenever we do something outside our comfort zone, we go from being the expert to the student.

2. Distraction

Most goals require a level of discipline and routine. For businesses, we have company goals, but an emergency or "fire" occurs and distracts us from doing the most important thing. As Stephen Covey mentions in his book, *First Things First*, we operate in 4 quadrants:

- Important/Urgent
- Important/Not Urgent
- Not Important/Urgent
- Not Important/Not Urgent

The area where goals are met with focus is in the quadrant of Important/Not Urgent. How do we do this? You might say this in unrealistic. I agree that we can't stop distractions and repetitive crises overnight. When we are in a crisis, we need to reflect on what caused it and determine how to fix the underlying problem.

3. Not SMART

All goals should be **S**pecific, **M**easurable, **A**ctionable, **R**ealistic, and **T**ime-bound. As mentioned above, Michael Hyatt adds exciting and relevant in his course. Most people make the goal very achievable and this can prevent us from stretching ourselves. There should be an element of risk to push us to accomplish more than before. One of the main problems is with the time-bound component. The key is to break down the goal into smaller daily and weekly chunks that are reviewed which makes the timing much more feasible and less stressful.

4. Lack of Accountability or Discipline

Accountability can come in many forms. Companies have executive teams, board members, and stockholders. Individuals have accountability groups, fitness trainers, friends and spouses. I think one of the most effective forms of accountability is discipline and routine. By setting up a daily routine, we form a new habit.

5. Unforeseen Events or Challenges

What happens if there is a layoff, sickness, injury, or financial challenge that prevents us from hitting our goal? We have to adjust. Goals are not set in stone. We should revise them and update them so they are reasonable and based on the latest situation. We should be careful not to say something is an unforeseen challenge when it is simply a recurring fire, issue, or distraction. If something is truly unforeseen, we need to adjust and rewrite our goals.

How to Avoid Goal Self-Sabotage

Have you wanted to accomplish a key goal, but something, someone, or yourself sabotages your goal? Do you let the opinions of others affect the accomplishment of your dreams? Here are some ideas to keep you on track.

1. Stay Focused

John Lee Dumas in his podcast, *Entrepreneur on Fire*, consistently says that FOCUS stands for Follow One Course Until Success. We have to stay focused and not let other people, ideas, or methods for doing something sabotage us. For example, have you started on a project and then had someone tell you about a new software, idea, or strategy to accomplish the project? Then you nearly scrap everything and start the new method. I had this happen twice with a goal to create an online course for small businesses.

My thought is that if you have a dream goal and you desire to accomplish it, you have to stay on the path until success. I am not saying that we won't learn as we go, but we should be very careful that we stay moving in the direction to meet the goal.

Do not think or do anything without having some aim in sight; the person who journeys aimlessly will have labored in vain. St. Mark the Ascetic

2. Mental Abundance

It is easy as we get older to get more cynical and have a hard time believing we can accomplish our dreams. I know that I have had others tell me that I am a certain way, and eventually I tell myself that this is simply the way I am. It is easier to be cynical and say that there won't be enough money or that something bad will happen (Murphy's Law).

The much more exciting and enjoyable way to live is to think abundantly. Michael Hyatt in "Your Best Year Ever" says abundance thinkers express gratitude, are happy to share, desire to learn more, are more optimistic, and think bigger.

3. Repetition and Review

In *The Freedom Journal*, I remember writing my goal each day for 100 days. I certainly didn't forget it. In Michael Hyatt's *Full Focus Planner* he recommends reading your goals daily to remember the key motivations for accomplishing the goals. The motivations are important in solidifying the goal in your mind so that a fleeting moment, distraction, or bad advice does not sabotage your goal.

4. Ask Why and then Ask Why Again and Again

Why do you want to accomplish the key goal? For example, I have a goal to read quality personal development books for 30 minutes a day for at least five days a week. Why do I want to do this? I want to continue developing myself so that I am more productive, efficient, and so I can provide more value to my clients. Why do I want to do this? If I add more value to my clients, they will be more successful, and so will I. Why do I want to do this? If both my clients and I are more successful, I can influence more people and our businesses will grow.

I could continue breaking down the whys and ultimately, for me, the cause would be a desire to serve more people in less time with the gifts God has given me.

In Ray White's book *Connecting Happiness and Success*, he says knowing your higher purpose helps you understand why your actions are meaningful and leads you in the right direction. This higher purpose gives you focus, motivation, and energy.

What is your key goal and why does it matter? What does it make possible and how does the accomplishment of this goal lead to other important possibilities?

5. People Can Help or Hurt

In Michael Port's book *Steal the Show*, he says "I coach and advise many aspiring speakers, CEOs, authors, and others, and they find it helpful to realize that they ultimately have to choose between results and approval." You can't really worry about the approval of others because there will always be someone with limiting beliefs who can bring you down. Maybe they don't want you to get hurt and they think they are helping. Maybe they tried and failed and can't see how you can do it when they could not. It is important to find the right people to surround yourself with to accomplish your goals.

I remember when starting my business a couple of years ago, I strongly believe that God put the right people around me at the right time. I remember being surprised at the encouragement I experienced, and this is a major reason that the business succeeded. So be sure to listen to the best podcasts, read encouraging books, and connect with others.

To be successful, you must be willing to do the things today others won't do in order to have the things tomorrow others won't have. – Les Brown

Something will happen to throw you off course and you will want to resort back to what is comfortable. Instead of going back, let's all stay focused, think abundantly, review our goals, ask why, and put the right people around us for success.

Call to Clarity

What is something that you do that sabotages your goals? Recognize it and choose one method to help you stay on track.

PART 4

ASSESS & ADJUST

Now, let's say you now know where you are today, and you know your destination. You also know and have implemented ways to get to your destination faster. Now what do you do? As with any journey, you always look at where you are compared to your goal. It requires a regular routine of reviewing your finances on a monthly and quarterly basis. There will be times to adjust, usually on a quarterly basis. What does adjustment look like in a financial sense?

As business owners and entrepreneurs, we have a tendency to adjust too quickly and often. It is one of the benefits of being a small business, but it can also be a curse. If we keep shifting our attention to the latest fad or shiny new object, it will be difficult to reach our specific destination. We will look back at the quarter and year and wonder what we actually accomplished. Yes, I know this is frustrating. Since we are talking about financial concerns, this may mean our business has not grown like we had hoped. We might be struggling with cash flow. We might have overspent in an area where we didn't plan to, and now we have to get out of a hole. It happens to all of us, even us financial guys. Don't beat yourself up. We learn from our mistakes.

In this section, we will work on ways to keep yourself more accountable through reporting mechanisms that will help you keep score. We will discuss how to see this by looking at your financials and also assessing your goals. We will look at a dashboard template that is helpful to stay on track no matter the size of your business. Finally, we will discuss other tools including journaling, white boarding, accountability groups, and helpful mentors.

CHAPTER 18

KEEPING SCORE

You have probably heard the expression "flying blind" and maybe you have seen it used in the broad context of doing something by guesswork with no instructions. It turns out this phrase dates back to World War II when the visibility for pilots was so bad they couldn't see the horizon, and therefore they had to rely on instrumentation to guide them through. I am not a pilot, but I can imagine that flying an airplane in a storm would be very challenging. But what if you were "flying blind" without instruments? Well, that would be considered suicidal.

As a business owner, have you ever wondered where your cash was going? Have you stayed awake at night wondering how much new business you needed to get or if you should hire someone or lay people off? How do you make such hard decisions? If you are operating without a good forecasting model, then this is even worse than "flying blind." You are flying blind with no instruments and with no guidance to help you maneuver the unknown.

One of the first things I do for any business I have worked with is to put together a forecasting model so that I am no longer flying blind. Here are some key components to this model:

Revenue/Sales

Understanding the drivers to what generates revenue and sales is the first step in building a good model. It is challenging to forecast much else without understanding the key service or product lines, revenue streams, or even contract terms. For example, in digital marketing, the revenue streams could be agency fee percentage of media, a monthly retainer, or even a markup based on the number of clicks or impressions (per 1,000 views) on a site.

Forecasting revenue and sales needs to be updated on at least a monthly basis based on new business, trending, and changes in the industry or economy. A good revenue forecast can even be beneficial to understand if everything has been billed in accordance to a contract, specifically with service-oriented clients.

Expenses

There are so many types of expenses that should be forecasted with different drivers (the cause of the expense). Understanding the drivers is essential in building a forecasting model that gets adjusted when variables change. For example, if revenue and sales change, then cost of goods sold or cost of service should change based on the historical margin for the business, product, or service. In most service businesses, the big expense is personnel costs, which is directly related to revenue. One method that I find effective is understanding the amount of revenue per person you expect per month for a particular service line, and then adding a new employee to the model once revenue increases to a new level. This makes scenario analysis easier because as revenue changes in the model, the personnel costs are automatically adjusted. So many costs can be attributed to personnel such as office supplies, travel, depreciation, training costs, and telecommunications. Some costs such as rent, software, or advertising might not have a direct correlation to personnel, at least in the short term, so they may need to be forecasted based on another method.

In summary, the most effective forecasting model is not hard coded line by line. It is based on key drivers that affect all the numbers when those drivers change. This will allow for versatile scenario analysis so that the executive team can make quick decisions.

Once sales/revenue and expenses are forecasted, then we can put together a good Income Statement. Please don't only focus on EBITDA (Earnings Before Interest, Taxes, Depreciation, and Amortization). EBITDA is a good Key Performance Indicator (KPI) but it is missing some important components in forecasting the Balance Sheet and subsequently, Cash.

Balance Sheet

I don't want to get too complicated, but I need to address the Balance Sheet. We can't understand where the cash is going or forecast where it will go without a good Balance Sheet forecast. Once again, key drivers are important. Accounts Receivable is a component of sales and collections. Accounts Payable is a component of costs of goods sold, operating costs, and any other vendor costs. Prepaid Expenses, Inventory, Accrued Liabilities, Fixed Assets, and Equity are all important to forecast based on trends and key industry metrics.

Statement of Cash Flow

Once the Income Statement and Balance Sheet have been forecasted, then the Statement of Cash Flow can be created based mostly on formulas. A typical Statement of Cash Flow is separated by operating, investing, and financing activities. The operating activities are typically a component of the income, depreciation, and current assets and liabilities (those items less than a year old). The investing activities are typically purchases of fixed assets or long-term investments. Finally, financing activities show cash flow related to debt and/or owner withdrawals/dividends.

Key Performance Indicators (KPIs) and Graphs

Most businesses typically have key measurements they like to see on a regular basis. Some KPIs could be for following:

- Gross margin percentage
- Operating margin percentage
- Revenue per person
- Revenue by service/product
- Margin by service/product
- Revenue growth over prior year, budget, and last forecast
- Profit growth over prior year, budget, and last forecast

A good dashboard with the main KPIs is very helpful for management to review everything in one place.

Sometimes creating a graph can tell a story much faster than numbers. Showing trends of revenue compared to last year versus budget can be helpful to understand changes in the business. If graphs show many ups and downs, consider smoothing it by looking at a rolling three-month or twelve-month view. Be sure not to rely on only one graph because it could be misleading. Develop a set of multiple revenue, expense, and profit graphs that clarify the direction the company is going and what needs to be done to improve.

A forecasting model is an essential tool that a business needs to navigate through the challenges of an unclear horizon. The forecasting model should be versatile with key drivers that can be easily adjusted to review different scenarios as the business changes. When the path is uncertain, you might have to "fly blind" with just the instruments to lead you through the cloudy path ahead. Without a forecasting model, you are not only flying blind, but deaf, naked, and invisible with no direction or plan for what lies ahead. With a forecasting model, at least you have some reasonable guidance to direct you to a safe landing.

• • •

One year I decided to be an assistant basketball coach for my 2nd grade twin boys' team. They didn't keep score on the scoreboard, but my players kept asking me who was winning. Of course, I told them that it didn't matter, and the most important thing was that they learn how to play the game. That didn't stop them from trying to keep score.

The next year I coached the 3rd grade team, and they did keep score on the scoreboard. Our team was losing by 20 points, so the referee asked if I wanted to turn off the scoreboard, but I told him "No." It was embarrassing, but the score was a strong motivator. At the time, I told the two players on the bench that we needed to try to score 8 more points. We stopped focusing on how badly we were losing, and instead began focusing on scoring one goal at a time, and we ended up scoring 12 more. We didn't win the game, but we won the 2nd half.

Keeping score is often not fun when you aren't winning or when your business is not growing as fast as desired. When building a financial forecasting model for your business, it is best to determine the key performance indicators (KPIs) that you want to track and to focus on them. A good forecasting model helps you maneuver throughout the changing business environment. KPIs are a key component of this forecasting model because they are your score. They help you know if you are improving, and they can provide additional motivation and excitement for your team.

Have I convinced you yet? I think for some of you, the acronym "KPI" puts you to sleep. Therefore, I have come up with five reasons that you need to review KPIs regularly in your business.

1. If You Can't Measure, It Isn't a Goal

One of the key components in setting and meeting your goals is to make sure they are measurable. I am guessing that you have a revenue and profit target, but is that specific enough? Once the revenue is broken down by product, service line, customer, location, or any other profit center, it is a KPI that should be measured.

2. How Do You Know That What You are Doing Today is Relevant?

In an *EO Fire* Podcast, Jordan Harbinger mentioned that when we focus on what is relevant, then we know we are doing the activities that are most important to hitting our goals. This seems kind of simple as I write it, but it is also profound. If we have a goal to hit a certain amount of new revenue, but we fill our day with distractions that don't help us achieve that goal, then we can get into trouble. If we are trying to get five new clients, then we should measure contacts, pitches, RFPs (Request for Proposals), referrals, close rate, etc., so we can adequately measure what we are doing to hit the new revenue goal and adjust if necessary.

3. I Didn't Make This Up

Measuring and reviewing KPIs is nothing new. In fact, it is a best practice among all kinds of businesses. I read a LinkedIn article by Bernard Marr called "The 75 KPIs Every Manager Needs to Know." It is a very thorough list broken down by financial, customer, marketing, operational, employee performance, and environmental categories. I wouldn't advocate every company tracking 75 KPIs as all are not applicable to every industry or goal. Even 5 or 10 KPIs will be helpful. Sometimes even one KPI can drive the point home. Remember the example of Revenue Per Head by month. This metric I use can help with hiring, pricing, and productivity improvements.

4. It's Fun

I know that I am a bit of a numbers nerd, so this might seem like a ludicrous statement to you. Why do I say it is fun? If we actually have a benchmark, and we communicate this to our team and we exceed it, how much fun is that? It is so much more fun to celebrate hitting the milestone that everyone set out to hit. Some of you might say that if you don't hit a goal, then it is depressing and could hurt employee morale. That might be the case in the short term, but if you have laser focus and work hard and hit the goal later, how much better is that for morale?

5. It Keeps You Out of Trouble

Measuring KPIs and comparing them to prior months or industry benchmarks can point you in the right direction or keep you from running into a financial challenge. If you have a loan with bank covenants, then you have KPIs that need to be measured and forecasted. If working capital or the debt to equity ratio is forecasted to fall below a bank covenant, then you know an adjustment needs to be made or you will be in a cash crunch.

In a service-oriented company, what if you are trying to decide on hiring an employee, but you notice that revenue per headcount is dropping? This trend might indicate that there are inefficiencies in place or client contracts that might need to be amended due to increased demands by the client.

If you notice that your average days of collection are increasing, then you know you could be in for a cash challenge. Maybe something has changed in the collection process or a large client is running into cash problems, so it is important to address these issues quickly.

In summary, KPIs in a financial model are important because they ensure we are measuring our goals and spending time on relevant activities. Further, utilizing KPIs is a best practice that can serve as a fun way to boost morale and keep your business out of trouble.

Call to Clarity

Pick at least one key performance indicator that you want to start reviewing regularly. Make sure it is something that you easily track and will be motivating and helpful in your business.

CHAPTER 19

BUSINESS DEVELOPMENT PLAN

Business owners, freelancers, and solopreneurs are growing. A Forbes article, "Why Small Business Ownership will Skyrocket in 10 years Especially by Solopreneurs" gives reasons for astonishing growth. "Intuit Research Reveals Five Trends Shaping the Future of Small Business" claims that U.S. small business over the next decade will grow from 30 million in 2016 to over 42 million in 2026. Another study mentioned in a Fast Company article, "Here's Why The Freelancer Economy Is On The Rise", states that by 2020, more than 40% of the American workforce will be independent workers which include business owners, freelancers, contractors, and solopreneurs.

There are many reasons to be a business owner. You can make more money, have a more flexible work schedule, do more of the work you love, and make a much larger impact in your area of expertise.

Why Business Development is So Important

I have read the statistics that most businesses fail for many different reasons. In the book *The 10X Rule*, Grant Cardone argues that you should set your goals 10 times larger than you think you can reasonably accomplish. This flew in the face of much of what I think. His reasoning is that by setting a goal this high, the level of excitement and focus will increase significantly. Your goals will get accomplished faster and you will be more prepared for all the negative surprises that could happen. I agree that having an aggressive goal is much more exciting and pushes you further than a small goal does.

There are many things out of our control. Think of 2008-2010 and how that affected so many businesses that weren't prepared. Keep working on business development and growth to significantly increase your chances of success and making a bigger impact.

I know that many people think working for one employer with benefits is the safer route to go. I certainly thought that way until I was laid off and went from a six-digit income with benefits to nothing. With a one-income household and four kids, my one source of income was a bit riskier than I thought.

A good product or service doesn't necessarily bring customers. Why do you see excellent restaurants go out of business? From my experience, sometimes a good service or product does better than an excellent product or service. Why is this? Think of McDonalds. Do they have the best hamburgers out there? Probably not. Maybe they have the best fries, but that is debatable. Their main strength is that they are very process oriented and people know what to expect each time. Their level of service and the cleanliness of their stores helps them. An organization that is strategic, manages cash flow, and adds value to their clients will grow and be successful.

How to Develop New Business

In one job as a financial advisor, I discovered that there were many ways to perform business development. I would meet with one mentor and he would tell me to go door-to-door to businesses in the morning between 7-8 am. He told me to bring donuts to the receptionist. Then after 8 am, I could go into the neighborhoods and just knock on doors. I found that one out five people would answer the door. It was grueling in September in Texas. I would wear my suit and tie and sweat to death in the near 100-degree heat. I remember one time I literally knocked on 100 doors in a row and nobody answered.

Then, I met with another mentor who told me that the best place to get contacts was to go to the mall or an event where there were many people and just go up and start talking to them. How nerve-wracking! One time when I was in a restaurant I started talking to a family eating lunch to introduce myself and the services I offered. I bet they thought that was annoying. There they were eating lunch as a family, and I was interrupting them.

One person told me to always shake hands and another said never shake hands. Other people told me to get involved in Chamber events and some told me not to. One person tried to recruit me to his firm when I knocked on his door. He told me that it is all about telephone cold calling because you can call more people. My head was spinning. I didn't know what to do. The best advice I heard when the stress and anxiety was getting overwhelming was to just be yourself and do what works best for you.

Business Development is important for any business to grow. The challenge is that there are so many opinions and ways to do it. How do we know what we should do? Since I started my own business, I have studied, tested, researched and come up with ways that work for me. That doesn't mean that I don't go through dry spells (remember the 100 houses). It simply means that you have to develop your business for it to grow.

What does it mean to develop your business? It really is about building relationships and following up and then following up again. The amount of follow-up can be quite significant. I have heard that you must average seven contacts or more with each prospect before you get their business. The most important thing is to simply have a business development plan that works well for your industry, your personality, and your business. You have to be consistent at working the plan.

I think most people know that you need to spend time developing your business for it to grow. The question is, do you truly believe it? For example, we all know that we should work out, and most of us know *how* to work out. We could even hire a trainer to have a more effective and efficient workout. The problem is, do we really believe working out will make us healthier, give us more energy, and improve our mental clarity? If you know you should work out but aren't doing it, how much do you believe that it works?

The same approach works with business development. I know that it is important, but sometimes I get too busy with clients or family and I just don't do it. Sometimes I am too tired or fear more rejection. Do I believe it works? How can I believe it so much that I make it a higher priority?

In Stephen Covey's Book *The 7 Habits of Highly Effective People*, he discusses a decision matrix of what is important and urgent. Dwight Eisenhower created the following:

Figure 19.1: Eisenhower Decision Matrix

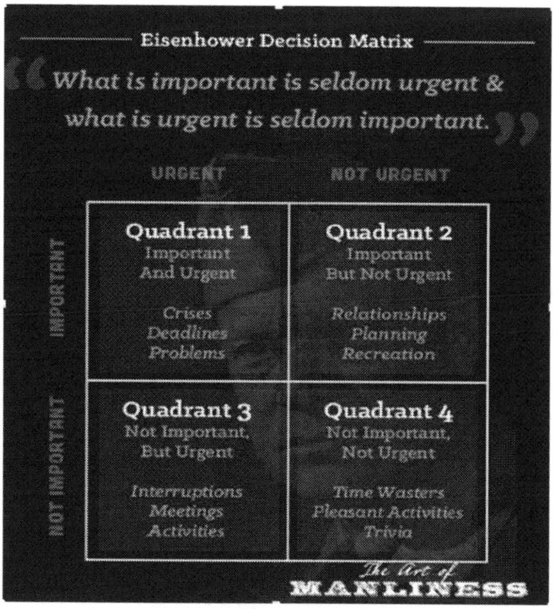

We tend to spend too much time in Quadrant 1, which is the Important and Urgent. Most of the time Business Development is Important but not Urgent and we struggle to get to it. Now if you are running out of cash or have lost a key customer, then Business Development might be in Quadrant 1. But we should not let a problem get to that level. We should always be doing it.

Let's go through a list of ways to develop business so you can decide what works best for you.

Physical Networking Events

Physical Networking Events include any kind of event that involves meeting people face-to-face. The goal is to meet as many people as quickly as possible, exchange business cards, and hopefully connect more with them later.

These events can be conferences, Chamber of Commerce meetings, MeetUp.com events, happy hour meetings, etc. I have found that you can spend quite a bit of time going to these events. I have had some people tell me they were great, and others say they were a waste of time. My experience has been mixed. There have been many meetings that have been helpful if I follow-up with the contacts and maybe schedule lunch or coffee to know them better. You never know if one of them will become a referral partner or a client/customer. My first client came from meeting a tax CPA through a chamber event. Just be careful about how much time you spend going to these events. Make sure you have a somewhat quick path to get to a decision maker for your ideal client/customer.

Online Networking

When I started my business, I spent quite a bit of money on a course to show me how to network through LinkedIn and Facebook. The process can work through any social media platform. Here are the steps:

1. Consistently post articles to keep your name and brand top of mind on social media. Use aggregator websites like Feedly.com.

2. Create a group with a logo and invite as many people as possible.

3. Use the filter capability to find potential clients. LinkedIn has a very powerful tool to find the right people.

4. Send out invites to as many people as possible. If your profile is set up right and you reach out at the right time, you can get 30-40% to connect.

5. Once they connect, invite them to your group.

6. Over the next few weeks, send them content that they will find helpful either through other sources or your own.

7. Develop a lead magnet (tool, paper, product) for them to opt in.

8. After about five or six messages, ask them for a quick phone call. By now it is not a cold call, and you come across as an expert in your industry.

Eventually you hope the phone call turns into business. Whether you get business or not, at the very least, you are at the front of their minds and you gradually build a network to market. It does build your list, connections, and Facebook friends. As with anything though, the more you work it, the better you get and the more likely you are to get business. It is time-consuming, and you can pay other firms to do this for you if you don't have the time and can afford it. It is worth giving it a try. If you get enough business from it, then keep on doing it.

Sales Funnels and Lead Generation

I have found this process to be the most fascinating. Typically, you start with a lead magnet that gets people on the email list. You can advertise on Facebook or Google. The recommendation is to give away some of your best advice for free. I know this varies by industry, but it is quite effective in the services industry. Over time, you sell them an inexpensive course or book. Then you eventually sell something more expensive such as your consulting or product.

The effectiveness of this strategy comes down to marketing and the value of the product. In *Dotcom Secrets* Russell

Brunson discusses the value ladder and how to effectively transition to more expensive and valuable products. He makes a comment that he heard from Dan Kennedy that "a buyer is a buyer is a buyer." This means that if they buy something small, then they are psychologically going to be more likely to buy something more expensive if it is valuable to them.

Friends and Family Network

The Friends and Family method is the easiest method as it simply means you reach out to your current friends and family. You can do this by email, text, phone, or face-to-face. The goal is to talk to them one-on-one. Most likely this method does not turn into big business, but there is a secret. You have to ask them one important question. "Can you give me three names of someone you know who might be interested in my service or product?" Then ask them for an introduction through email, social media or in person. As you can imagine, you can really increase the number of warm leads this way.

Cold Calling: Phone or Door-to-Door

Cold Calling is typically calling someone via the phone or knocking on the door of someone you haven't met or been introduced to. In my opinion, this is the hardest kind of sales. It is a numbers game, so the more people you contact, the more customers you will have. The goal is to have a good script, perfect it, and be genuine. Also, you probably don't want to be pushy. When going door to door, I found the conversation went the best if I could figure out some way to quickly connect to them. Do they have kids near your kids' ages or did they go to the same college? You can be most successful when you are consistent, authentic, and believable.

No matter if you focus on one method above or some of each of them, the most important thing is to focus on your actions. It is difficult to control getting people to buy from you. It is important to ask for the sale, but you can't make them say yes. If you are pushy, then it is counterproductive and will hurt you in the future. You can control your actions which means you can always connect with more people. The goal with any business development plan is to learn as you go and figure out how to add as much value to as many people as you can in the least amount of time.

Tools to Help with Prospecting

You will probably find that you will meet many people, but merely meeting others does not turn into new business that easily. You have to follow-up. I have had some clients close with only a couple of meetings or phone calls and others that have taken over six months of follow-up. Timing is very important. At first, I used Excel to keep track of everyone, but that is not a good long-term solution. I use Vipor to keep track of contacts because it is affordable and works well with my iPhone and Mac. Other good, affordable solutions are Zoho, Contactually, and Salesforce.

There really is no lack of affordable software solutions to help you stay organized. You just need something that will help you categorize your contacts, help you keep notes about important conversations, and remind you to follow-up. You also need to block time on your calendar each week to work on business development.

Call to Clarity

Block out time each week for business development. Try something new and come up with a weekly plan that you can implement that will keep new opportunities coming to your business.

CHAPTER 20

GOALS ASSESSMENT

When my daughter was four years old, she had a goal. She wanted to go six nights with a dry pull-up. I asked my wife where six nights came from and she said that six nights was about a week. Last I checked, a week is seven days, so I guess she is going to take the seventh day off. One morning she really wanted to inform me that she had to start over because she had a wet pull-up. She looked at me with an innocent smile on her face and said, "I am starting another 6 days." I thought about that some and decided it gives good insight for assessing and adjusting goals. Most of us don't have to start over completely as goals change and adjust, but we should be willing to adjust and reset our time schedule.

How do we assess our measurable goals, and when do we readjust? Below are five action steps when assessing and readjusting our goals.

1. Do Not Give Up

Most people will give up when they don't meet their goals. If you have a business, most likely you really don't have this option. One way you might give up is to stop measuring your progress or communicating with employees. I remember working with a company that seemed to communicate to employees in monthly meetings when we were exceeding our revenue targets. But when we stopped exceeding the revenue goals, they took that out of the presentation as if people didn't question what was happening. I think this is a form of giving up. The company and team need to know what is going on with regards to goals.

2. Assess Monthly and Adjust Quarterly

You should assess your goals on a monthly basis, but avoid making large changes quickly. On a quarterly basis, it is good to make adjustments so that goals remain reasonable.

If you have a service business in which you have prospects and clients, you should have a pipeline report that compares to your goals. You should assess all prospects and give them a probability of closing. In Chapter 8, I wrote about the following guidance I have used in the past:

- 25% Probable – Early discussions with a prospect, but you have an idea about potential revenue.

- 50% Probable – Pitching a prospect with more serious intentions.

- 75% Probable – At this point, you are probably talking about contract terms and have received some indications of significant interest.

- 90% Probable – Contracts are sent and awaiting legal and signature.

- 100% – Signed agreement

At least on a monthly basis, you should be assessing the revenue pipeline. You should be able to calculate the prorated revenue in the pipeline report and see a reasonable way to meet the goal. On a quarterly basis, the revenue goal should be adjusted based on the latest pipeline report.

3. Short-Term Memory

If a goal is not working and you need to go down another path, have a short-term memory. I know this seems like you should forget your mistakes, but that is not what I am saying. It is just not helpful to dwell on the past. It is a waste of energy and creativity to keep thinking about your last goal or plan that didn't work. For a start-up or very young business, adjusting or completely going in another direction is common.

4. Communication with Others

At least once a month, I meet with a group of five leaders and business owners to discuss goals and hold each other accountable. We get personal, pray for each other, and lean on the differing experiences and talents of everyone in the group.

A while back I met Rod at a McDonalds and started meeting with him regularly. We got to know each other better, and he actually asked if he could mentor me. I had never been asked this question. At the time when I met him, he was 82 years old with a vast amount of experience as an entrepreneur and in sales. I have enjoyed being mentored. Accountability and mentorship are essential for success.

5. Assess What Is and Isn't Working

I know this probably seems intuitive. If something isn't working, then we should probably stop doing it. The challenge is figuring out when to stop doing something. Often, most people are so busy that they forget to think and strategize.

A while back, I created a Life Plan from the book *Living Forward*. The benefit of having a Life Plan is to assess when you're getting off course. In many cases, a plan may not be materializing because we are either veering off course or we aren't doing the things we need to do to be successful.

Ways to Assess and Adjust Your Financial Goals

As a business owner, you have financial goals. You desire more revenue, customers, products, or profit. The problem is that it doesn't happen the way you think. As mentioned before, a quarterly assessment and adjustment is necessary. So, what do you do during this time? In Michael Hyatt's book *Best Year Ever*, he suggests going through at least three steps before you remove your goal or replace your goal with something else.

First of all, we should celebrate the accomplishments in this quarter. Many times, we have done more than we think.

Second, if the goal is important, then we must recommit to it. For example, if you have a goal to hit a certain revenue target because this will allow you to hire more people, do more marketing, or launch a new product, then you have to figure out how to get to that revenue number.

Third, sometimes that financial goal needs to be revised. Revenue changes regularly. We get a new client or a big sale and now the revenue forecast goes up. We lose a client or business is sluggish, then we lower the forecast. I think it is exciting to have a high revenue goal, but we have to keep expenses in check with a revenue goal that isn't delusional. Also, if we are already tracking higher than the original goal, we should stretch ourselves and go for a higher goal to keep it exciting and challenging.

Finally, sometimes the goal may not be important, and something else is important. Now, financially it is likely that revenue and profits is not a goal that should be removed.

What may be the case is that you have to focus on developing a new product or getting educated on something, so you can rise above the competition. Maybe your processes are disorganized, and you struggle with bringing in more business until this is figured out. I personally think revenue should always be a goal, but it is the how and specifics of reaching that target that can change.

Call to Clarity

Take time to assess and adjust any goal that is not working. If you don't have any revenue or profit goal for your business, set one and develop a plan to reach this goal.

CHAPTER 21

THE FINANCIAL MODEL

Do you have a financial forecasting model in your business that is updated regularly?

In a call with a potential client, the owner asked how having a financial model would make them money so that they could pay for my services. I like this question because it gets down to the basics as a business owner.

After some more thought, here are the top 10 reasons all businesses need a working financial forecast in their business.

Reason 1: Make Quicker and More Informed Decisions

Decisions can be challenging to make. Waiting too long could prevent us from getting a good deal, hiring excellent talent, or getting ahead of the competition. If we make a bad decision, it could cost us time and money. In the book, *Creating Great Choices*, the authors state that we tend to seek the most direct and simplified approach in making decisions. We overestimate our reasoning and leadership ability which is filled with biases, limited experiences, and firm beliefs. A forecasting model is much more objective in showing you what is happening so your decisions are not skewed.

Reason 2: Helps You Save Money

Reviewing your finances regularly will show you areas that may be getting out of hand. Maybe you see an increase in an expense category. After reviewing it further, you realize you don't need it or you should find a less expensive option. It always seems like expenses just creep up. Your business insurance automatically goes up every year. Subscriptions pile up and sometimes we forget about them. Credit card processing fees also tend to increase.

Reason 3: Planning Your Revenue Brings More Revenue

We all know that more revenue growth cures many problems in your business and will lead to more profitability. The first step in the plan is to know how you are going to meet your revenue goals. How many new customers do you need to close? How are you going to get this business? The act of doing this exercise and then tracking will keep your marketing and business development at the front of your mind.

Reason 4: Consistency Makes Running a Business Easier

I suggest reviewing a rolling forecast of your business monthly and comparing actual results to the last forecast, budget, and last year if applicable. This consistent process will build momentum and understanding. You will gain energy and excitement when the business is doing well. When results fall below your goals, you have a process to keep working hard because you see the plan and possibilities.

Reason 5: Better Understanding of Cash Flow

Businesses run on cash flow. A better understanding of future cash flow will help you make decisions with hiring, advertising, and large purchases. It might even prevent you from needing a loan, which is very time consuming. You can also see, through a few tweaks, how your business could increase cash flow.

Reason 6: More Peace and Less Chaos (Priceless)

Almost everyone wants more peace in their lives and less chaos. Some people thrive on the adrenaline from chaos, but in the end, this becomes tiring. It leads to more stress and sickness and less sleep. Even though a forecast changes, you have a much better understanding of the direction of your business. You understand your results better and how decisions you make affect your revenue, profit, and cash flow. As you forecast more, you get better at forecasting a few months out.

Reason 7: Builds Team Consensus and Understanding

As your business grows, you need a way to communicate to your team so that everyone knows your goals. They need to be part of the forecasting process to understand what role they play. This builds empowerment, especially among the leaders in your company, so they can use their judgment to meet the financial goals you have.

Reason 8: More Awareness of Looming Issues

Growing a business always has some issues looming on the horizon. What if you could project this before it became a major fire? The goal of a good forecasting model is to identify these risks earlier so that you can address them before they become urgent. You have more control of the timing, rather than some cash flow or client service issues popping up on the worst possible day.

Reason 9: Helps Prioritize Challenges

Most likely there are many challenges such as cash flow, inventory, client service, and hiring. How do you know what to work on first? My suggestion would be to work on whichever one provides the biggest impact on your business based on revenue and profitability. You can see this more clearly in a good forecast model. This helps you make better decisions which saves you time and money.

Reason 10: Increases Flexibility and Decreases Overreaction

When you are in the dark about the financial challenges in your business, you can overreact. You check your bank balance and it is close to zero. A client doesn't get the service they require, so you build a story of catastrophe in your head. Overreaction is counterproductive for you and your team. You need flexibility and understanding as to what is really happening. Then, you can solve the most important problems and stay on track.

Therefore, as you can see with these 10 reasons, a financial forecast model is essential for financial success.

Common Business Owner Thinking

Are you having these thoughts right now?

- "I am too small to have a forecasting model."
- "Financial Models are for finance people and not relevant to me."
- "I don't know all the variables yet, so I will wait until I have more information."
- "This is a waste of time. I just need to bring in more business."
- "I don't have the time."
- "I don't know how to do this, and accounting reports such as these make no sense to me."

As I meet business owners, I am amazed at how many operate without a financial model. I wonder how they make decisions and how they have been or will be successful.

I will stress that a financial model is not the only thing needed for success. Obviously, you need marketing, operations, sales, a quality service or product, and a system to be successful and grow.

I have an answer for the six hesitations mentioned above. Let's go through them.

"I am too small to have a forecasting model."

You are never too small to have a good forecasting model. If you are a start-up, it is helpful to build out a model to understand all the variables needed for success. The act of building out the model will bring different expenses, revenue ideas, and cash flow requirements to the surface.

Before we move further, we need to make one thing clear. No matter how much time you spend on a model, it will not be right. It will be outdated as soon as you finish. It is not about being right. It is about having a plan formulated in your mind for success. The more you forecast, the more you understand your business, your customers, and the competition. You will get more accurate, but it will never be completely right.

"Financial Models are for finance people and not relevant to me."

Yes, there are some very complex financial models with complex formulas and assumptions. I have seen models that I have no idea how to manipulate or to draw conclusions. This is not what I am talking about. It can be as simple or complex as you want. If you keep churning the work without assessing what is working and looking at the numbers, you may be spending time in areas that aren't profitable. I suggest starting small and growing from there.

I am talking about reviewing your revenue and understanding key metrics such as revenue and margin by client or product. What business owner wouldn't want to know that?

Also, since nobody likes to waste money or time, this exercise serves to prevent this from happening. Eventually, you will better understand where you get the best profit for your time and investment. Understanding this will keep the cash flow going even as you invest in new technology, ideas, products, training, and research.

"I don't know all the variables yet, so I will wait until I have more information."

We are never going to know all the variables. Sometimes, we actually know very few variables. Usually, people know more than they think when they put it together in a model.

I can understand the desire for perfectionism, which many times leads to procrastination. I like the quote by the founder of LinkedIn, "if you are not embarrassed by the first version of your product, you've launched too late." In other words, if you if aren't embarrassed by your first financial forecast, you waited too long.

"This is a waste of time; I just need to bring in more business."

I totally get that analysis paralysis can keep you from doing anything. You could spend days on a financial model with multiple versions. I put together a model for a start-up and we had departments and then reference sheets that tied out to the departments. The totals of the departments tied to the Profit & Loss Statement (P&L). The Excel file got so complicated that one change in the model created hours of work. I realize you can set up a spreadsheet to prevent this, but you can also spend too many hours setting up a bullet proof spreadsheet that will probably get destroyed once someone hacks it and writes over a formula.

The point of a forecasting model is to quickly assess your revenue streams, expenses, profit, and cash flow. The information the model gives you can provide a sense of urgency or possibly less anxiety since you have a better understanding of what you need to accomplish to meet your financial goals.

"I don't have the time."

We all make time for what is important. A forecasting model is supposed to ultimately give you the focus and direction to use your time more productively. The financial plan and ongoing forecasts will allow you to measure your actual performance against goals, which is essential for success. Every quarter, you will need to pivot your goals and adjust.

"I don't know how to do this, and accounting reports such as these make no sense to me."

I understand that accounting reports can be confusing if you aren't familiar with them. If you are a business owner, it is in your best interest to understand the Income Statement, Balance Sheet, and Statement of Cash Flows. Accounting reports such as these are basic and help outside investors, bankers, CPAs, and other consultants and professionals better understand your business. Accounting is basically the language of business.

I am more passionate about using reports such as these to operationally grow the company. Use these reports if you want to:

- be more profitable.

- hire more people.

- increase the value of your company.

- manage growth.

- control your cash.

In summary, a forecasting model is essential to put together a framework of where you are now and where you are going in your business. There are many misconceptions about forecasting. No matter your size, no matter how much you know, no matter how much time you have, or even if you don't fully understand, it is essential to have a forecasting model that is updated regularly for your business.

Call to Clarity

If you do not have a forecast model for your business, get started as soon as possible. Look at Appendix 1 for more help or hire a professional. Make it easy to update with actual changes in your business.

CHAPTER 22

A USEFUL DASHBOARD

The car dashboard has been getting more complex and computerized in the last few years. When we purchased a Honda Odyssey for our large family, I had to figure out where to look. There were symbols, screens, and alerts for everything. It tells us when we need an oil change and when one of our tires is low. The lights come on when it gets dark, and a gas light comes on when we are nearly out of gas. My car even beeps when closing in too fast toward another car or going over the line.

In business, we fear failure. We fear losing clients or not having enough cash for payroll. We might fear paying taxes or not paying vendors and suppliers which affects our ability to do business. What if there was a way to alert us of potential failures? Just like when we are about out of gas or have low tires, we get notified when we are low on cash or maybe low on a product or inventory. It all depends on what is important in your business. Obviously, gas, tires, and oil are important for cars. Revenue, expenses, cash, and margins are important for your business. We need a financial dashboard to help us understand an issue that may be on the horizon, so that we can adjust quickly before we have a blowout, or our car ends up in the shop.

Let's go through five ways that a good dashboard can help any business.

1. Stay on Track of Goals

We have goals for revenue, profit, new clients, and margin. No matter what the goals are, we should regularly review actual results to these goals. I encourage at least a monthly review for any business. The dashboard will show you when you are off track. Then you can drill further to solve the problem before it is too late. It may be stressful when you are behind your goal, so I encourage you not to get angry or too emotional. Think about what you are going to do this week to get back on track. Focus on your actions.

Sometimes it is better to track the actions because they are more inside your control. You can track the number of phone calls, lunches, or proposals.

2. See Issues Before They are Urgent

What if you could tell there was going to be an issue before it happened? A good dashboard will give you red flags, so you can adjust. Wouldn't you sleep better at night knowing that your business numbers were trending in the right direction? Fear of the unknown is one of the strongest fears we have in business. Now, I am not saying that a dashboard will tell you everything. The further out you go in time, the more unknown everything is. You simply want to create a dashboard that gives you a head start on potential issues.

3. Know Where to Look

Have you ever felt like something was wrong, but you didn't know where the problem was coming from? Your bank account is telling you that you are running out of cash, but you don't know where to look. A good dashboard will quickly show you the area that requires more digging. One of my clients was not sure where the cash was going in his business, so we looked at a simple report that showed the cash flow details and quickly discovered the answer.

4. Saves Time

Have you ever been lost in the details of a project? Then you took a break and stepped back, and you saw the problem. It is easy to get lost in the weeds in a small business. Sometimes business owners are wearing multiple hats.

If you look at a weather radar, you may see rain all around your area. The next step would be to scroll out and see a larger area to understand how long the rain is going to last.

The dashboard provides you with a 30,000-foot view so you can more quickly make decisions on the most important priorities.

5. Understand Your Business Better

When you first start reviewing a dashboard, you might not know what the most important metrics are for your business. The more you review how your revenue, profit, and cash flow are related in your business, you will understand the financial aspects of your business better. Some of this comes with experience. You will begin to see trends in your business based on seasonality and marketing. These will be helpful to forecast the future.

I tend to use weather examples because I like weather. I read the forecast discussion that the meteorologists write for their forecast reasoning. They are always discussing different computer models which are based on historical information from over a hundred years of data. The amount of data is continually increasing which helps them improve their forecast. I know they have a long way to go, but they have improved their short-term forecasts in the last few decades.

The same is true for your business. The more data you have on your business, the better you understand how to increase revenue and profits at a faster pace.

Ideas for the Dashboard

So, what do you put in your dashboard? There are hundreds of metrics you could look at, but who has that kind of time? I will simplify this for you. Here are some ideas:

Important numbers to compare to Goal/Budget, Last Month, and Last Year

- Revenue/Sales
- Gross Margin %
- Expenses
- Operating Profit
- Operating Profit %
- Cash
- Headcount
- Revenue per person
- Revenue by service/product category

New Business

- Client Meetings
- New Business prorated by the probability of close.
- New Services

Marketing

- Website traffic
- Social Media followers, Shares, Likes, etc.
- Email List
- Results of any marketing promotion

Keep it Simple

Dashboards can get very complex with many ratios and trends that can be tracked. Just like when I first started driving the Odyssey, I didn't know where to look. It was almost dangerous because I was taking my eyes off the road for too long. Business Dashboards are meant to be easy to read and simple to use for decision making. I would suggest an easy dashboard with less than ten metrics and less than five graphs. Sometimes only one metric can tell the whole story better than anything.

The key is to take the time to review these numbers and then get back to work making your business dreams a reality.

Call to Clarity

Take the KPI that you decided was important in Chapter 18 and develop a quick dashboard. It might be a chart or a graph. Connect your dashboard to your financial model so it changes as your model changes. Once again, don't over-complicate it. A dashboard is best designed to be easy to read and understand.

CHAPTER 23

IDEAS TO STAY ON TRACK

Does the word "accountability" sound too challenging or threatening? Does it sound like too much work or too structured? One challenge as a business owner is finding people to discuss ideas or finding time to grow and invest in your own personal development. How do we do this when we stay busy all the time? In short, we really don't have time to not do this. We must invest in ourselves, or we could get burnt out, or the competition could wipe us out. We could be wasting time or missing out on revenue by not taking advantage of new technology or ways to get leads. The exciting thing is that these days there are so many affordable and flexible ways to do this.

Necessary Reports

Every business owner should review key reports to understand how they are doing financially. It is essential that the reports are close to the end of the previous month in order to take action and make adjustments as needed. Any accounting package will have an Income Statement and Balance Sheet. These reports will have more meaning if you compare them to your budget or plan for the year, last month, or last year. The Income Statement will give you an understanding of the revenue, expenses, and profit in your business. The Balance

Sheet gives you a snapshot of your cash, assets, liabilities, and equity in your business.

Depending on the size of your business there are many different metrics, reports, and dashboards that are helpful. At one of the companies I worked for, we had a simple metric that we used to determine hiring and ensure we remained profitable. We simply wanted to run the company so that revenue averaged $17,000 per head per month. We knew our break even, and this was an easy metric to calculate and make decisions.

Goals and Journaling

Another form of accountability is writing down goals and journaling. I realize some people have trouble doing this. We instantly think of New Year's resolutions. Many of us write down goals and never look at them again. Try using *The Freedom Journal* to help. When I started my business, I had a 100-day goal to get to a certain amount of sustainable revenue. There were numerous distractions that started to take me off course, but the journal brought me back. As mentioned in Chapter 17, this journal requires that you write down the following each day:

- What am I grateful for?

- The 100 Day goal

- Number One Focus for the Day

- Three things I am going to do to help me hit my goal

- Action plan for the day

- At the end of the day, write down two accomplishments

- Then, write down two struggles and solutions
- Write down how tomorrow is going to be great

Habits

We all have habits, but how do we increase our good habits? I realize there are books written on this. A great one is *The Power of Habit* by Charles Duhigg. One thing Duhigg suggests is that our willpower decreases throughout the day. Whatever we want to accomplish that is hard or challenging should be accomplished earlier in the day.

I was listening to a podcast on *The Ziglar Show* and they were interviewing Joshua Spodek and discussing Self-Imposed, Daily, Challenging, Healthy Activities (SIDCHAs). These habits could be many different things from exercises like burpees to writing, reading, prayer/meditation, and much more. When I heard this, I started doing burpees which are quite tiring, but an effective exercise to do.

Also, Michael Hyatt has a course called "Free to Focus" that he offers where he discusses having a Morning Routine. Some activities I include in my routine are the following:

- Drink a glass of water and cup of coffee

- Read the Bible

- Prayer and meditation

- Journal – See *The Freedom Journal* by John Lee Dumas as mentioned above or the *Full Focus Planner* by Michael Hyatt.

- Exercise and listen to a podcast or read at the same time (I like the treadmill or elliptical for this).

- Usually, I drink a smoothie filled with protein and vitamins.

Personal Development

I am a fan of personal development. I realize sometimes it can get overwhelming to read enough books or listen to all the podcasts. Today it is easier because there is so much content at our fingertips. There are online courses that can be taken at any time. I have heard that you should spend 3-5% of your budget on training and personal development. Therefore, I will give you five reasons why you should invest time on personal development:

1. Podcasting and audio books are easy and inexpensive and are much more fulfilling than talk radio.

2. Online courses can be taken at night and on weekends. Many of them have 30-day money back guarantees.

3. Technology and the world are changing fast, so you need to invest in yourself.

4. Learning just one good idea to increase revenue, save time, or save expenses is well worth it.

5. Learning builds confidence and increases your value to your customers and network.

Groups and Coaching

Finally, sometimes we need others to help us become better than we are. I have personally struggled with spending the money on a business coach, but I can see the value. There are mastermind groups and other networks that can support you. I do think that much of the accountability comes with your own desire for commitment and improvement. You can spend money on coaches and groups, but you have to find time to implement the change. Reviewing your financial reports, journaling, setting and reviewing goals, developing good habits and routines, and setting aside time for personal development will go a long way.

At the end of the day, we need to surround ourselves with the right people. This quote tells it all.

You are the average of the five people you spend the most time with. – Jim Rohn

Distractions

We are in the midst of an epidemic. The disease is getting worse with the ever-increasing technology and demands on our time and attention. People don't have time to think. Businesses don't have time to plan. People spend all day answering email, checking social media, and responding to group texts. The hours go by and the list gets longer. How can we stop this distraction epidemic?

I admit that I have been infected, and I am always looking for a cure. Remember the 1986 movie, *Ferris Bueller's Day Off*. The movie is still very enjoyable, but it is dated. There is a scene where Ferris is talking to freshmen on a pay phone (no cell phones). Back then computers were much more basic, there was no such thing as texting, and Facebook didn't exist. It was interesting that one of the themes of the movie is Ferris Bueller telling the audience to take the time to enjoy life and have fun.

What can we do to minimize distractions and focus on what is important? Here are five ideas:

1. Morning Quiet Time

For those who aren't morning people, you are missing out. There is so much greatness that can happen from 5-7am in the morning. I start the day in prayer and read the Bible. There is a reason it is the most published book in the world. According to the Guinness World Records, there may be as many as five billion Bibles published since the early 1800s. You can't argue that there isn't some wisdom and value that comes from reading it.

Prayer, meditation, and journaling are all extremely valuable at the beginning of the day. This activity helps me to be grateful, gain perspective, consider others, and ask God for wisdom.

Your journaling can include almost any writing you want. The most important thing is to write down three major activities to help you accomplish your most important goals. Put this on the calendar. Also, writing down something you are grateful for puts your day in the right perspective.

2. Exercise

I know this is not news to most people. The problem is that it is hard to exercise consistently. I would suggest coming up with a plan to do it every day or at least five to six days a week even if it is only for twenty minutes. We crave consistent routines, so once it is a built-in habit, you will feel like something is missing if you don't do it. My thought is that any exercise is better than no exercise. Sometimes we overdo it and workout for two hours, but this is not sustainable. It has to be an activity that is sustainable over the rest of your life.

3. Use Technology to Fight Technology

Unless we have an apocalyptic event soon, technology is probably not going away. We need to live with it. I think there is good and bad with everything. Cell phones, computers, Google, and social media are wonderful inventions if used correctly, but they can be easily misused. Here are some ideas:

- Utilize the "Do Not Disturb" function on your phone.

- Turn off email notifications.

- Use Focus@Will, a Spotify Playlist or something like these. Music can help you focus and block out distractions when doing something that requires all of your attention.

- Use an online calendar to time-block important meetings and activities.

- Listen to free podcasts on productivity, leadership, personal development, and success.

4. Schedule Time That Is Not Scheduled

We all need to have margin in our life that is not scheduled. This is a challenge for me. I try to leave Sunday afternoons open. I would probably recommend more time than this, but it all depends on what phase of life you are in. Those with young families and demanding jobs probably will have a bit less time than those who are not married, do not have kids or who are in the "golden years" of life.

In Michael Hyatt's book *Living Forward*, he talks about putting together a three-year plan. I am not saying that this plan must be set in stone. I am sure things will change. The point is to schedule big events such as holidays, anniversaries, and vacations. I am trying to spend individual time with each of my four kids, and I have these dates scheduled.

5. Enjoy God's Creation

There is something relaxing about being outside with fresh air and enjoying the beauty of God's creation. I have always found trips to the mountains or the beach to be relaxing. It can be as easy as taking a walk around the neighborhood or finding a state park to take a hike. Dr. Mercola mentions in an article that getting outside enhances creativity, focus, mood, and self-esteem.

New distractions will come along as technology advances. This is not necessarily a bad thing, but we need to be in control of our time and our attention. Make it a priority to have a morning quiet time, exercise, be smart with technology, schedule unscheduled time, and enjoy the outdoors.

Call to Clarity

Pick one good habit to implement and keep track of how you are doing. Habits take longer than you think to form so try doing it consistently over the next three months.

CHAPTER 24

NEXT STEPS TO GROWTH

In *Lead With a Story*, Paul Smith tells of the Fayetteville High School Basketball team that was not expected to do anything great. The team was made up of juniors. In the last half of the season, the team started to win games closely at the end. The Bulldogs started playing well together and the momentum took them to the playoffs. During the playoffs, their success continued, and they started to win games by double-digit margins. They started to believe they could have a shot at the state title.

The state title game was a real David and Goliath matchup and almost straight out of the movie *Hoosiers*. The game was very close and went to double overtime. With 15 seconds left in the game, the Fayetteville Bulldogs had the ball and the coach called a timeout. Their star player had not made many mistakes, so this point guard was to hold the ball until the clock ran down to five seconds and then he would start the play. The mistake was that he let his defender get too close for too long without passing, and they lost possession. The other team's star player drove down to the basket and was fouled, and he made his free throws. The Fayetteville Bulldogs had gotten so close, but they lost.

At the end of the game, one of the players was being interviewed about the game and he nonchalantly said, "No big deal. We are all juniors. We'll be back next year and win it for sure." This is the kind of advice parents say to a child after a bitter loss and the whole team started repeating this mantra within hours of the game.

The next year the whole starting line-up was back, and they were seniors. They were heavily favored and the team to beat. They won every game in the regular season and were the number one seed in the tournament. Unfortunately, in the first round the Bulldogs lost to a team they were heavily favored to beat. They had lost their chance. The seniors would be graduating. They would never get another chance to play in the state finals again.

I don't tell you this story to depress you, but to motivate you. When I first heard the story, it did make me sad, but it is true. There is not always another chance. Opportunities are lost all the time. The competition and the economy changes. The finances of a company change and we all get older.

Are you waiting until your finances get better or your business gets bigger to take control of your business finances? Are you waiting for some big breakthrough to finally take you to the next level? Are you waiting until you have more time to think strategically, enhance your marketing and business development efforts, or launch a new client?

First, do you know today where are you are financially? Do you have up-to-date billing, accounting, and financial reports and understand your cash situation today as compared to the previous month, quarter, or year?

Second, then do you know where you are going financially? Do you understand your revenue and expense trends and how that will translate into profits and ultimately cash flow? With this information, you are armed with getting a better understanding of your tax liabilities. You can better plan for investments, new products, or hiring.

Third, do you know how to get to your destination more quickly? Have you built in at least one new habit in your organization to instill discipline? Have you looked at using consistency and automation to build the systems needed to scale and grow? I know this is not the easiest thing to do as it requires change management many times. Often, one small habit change can create a domino effect of other opportunities and improvements that are hard to see, but which are essential for growth and competiveness.

Finally, do you have a system to keep yourself accountable, to assess your progress toward your financial goals, and to adjust when necessary? Do you have a rolling forecast with a dashboard to quickly assess how you are tracking? Have you scheduled time on your calendar to do this monthly and quarterly?

Don't feel bad if you have not accomplished some or most of these. This is very common, which is one of the main reasons I went into business providing these kinds of services. Although we can't fret over the past or what we should have done, we *can* look at how we are going to improve going forward. It can start with just one thing. The Bulldogs story shows you there is not always a next time. Sometimes you need to take control of the situation now as if you won't have another chance.

Think about your future business in 10 years. It is hard to really know this far ahead, but just think about it. You have a successful business that is growing and making a significant impact in the lives of your customers, employees, and the economy. You have built a scalable business that does not require you to keep it running. You are influencing others, but have time for your family, hobbies, spiritual life, and other dreams. What if you can look back to this moment that changed everything? It was then that you became more intentional. It reminds me of the first *Back to the Future* when Marty McFly came back from being in 1955 and his father was now a successful author and his mom was trim and healthy. It all went back to the moment in time in 1955 when his father faced his fears and made changes. I know this is a movie, but we know a single moment in time can make a difference in the future.

I heard Zig Ziglar say once, "Do you believe in the next week you can do something to make your life worse?" Everyone nodded their heads "Yes." If you believe this, then the opposite is true, and you can do something in the next week, month, year, and 10 years to make your life better.

No matter if you are a start-up, a small growing business, you work in a business, or even if you work at a non-profit, you can start today to improve your financial situation. Don't miss the opportunity.

Call to Clarity

Pick one thing that you are going to do in the next day to help you positively impact the future in your business.

ACKNOWLEDGEMENTS

To everyone who believed in me and helped me accomplish this.

Holly Bender – My beautiful wife, prayer warrior, encourager, and supporter to keep going. Life is so much better with her by my side.

Steve & Debbie Bender, Seth Bender, & Heidi Cumbie – From growing up to starting and growing my business, you have always encouraged me, prayed for me, and been there for me.

Sons of Thunder Group (Iron Sharpens Iron) - Thank you for your support, prayers, and encouragement.

Kyle Gabhart, Christopher Haltom, Daniel Ogle, Justin Winstead

Mentors

Ray White, Rod Routen, Kary Oberbrunner & the Igniting Souls Tribe

Editors, Encouragers, Supporters, and Friends – This book is better because of your input and support. Thank you very much.

Matt Eagleston, Dwayne & Angelique Gates, Jason Noble, Mike Perkins, Mary Poling, Gene Wilkes

Freelancers

Trivuj – Cover design

Michele Stanford & The Guild – Professional Editor

To everyone who read my blog and sent encouraging notes which was the fuel that kept me going.

MECHANICS OF THE FORECAST MODEL

Throughout the book, I have provided guidance on why having a working forecast model is essential. So now what do you do? I have created a relatively simple Microsoft Excel template that you can use to start building your forecast model. Download templates at www.bendercfoservices.com/forecast-templates

I have also provided you a completed example which shows you better how the different tabs work together. This example forecast does require some knowledge of Microsoft Excel. If you feel uncomfortable, I strongly encourage you to find someone to help you, or even better, learn Excel so you can use the model as you make decisions going forward. It will certainly save you time. No matter what you do, don't let the technology scare you.

Step 1: Entry Tab

Put the name of your business which will flow through to other tabs in the spreadsheet.

The "First Month" is the month in which you want to start your forecast model. I suggest going back at least to the beginning of your previous fiscal or calendar year. If you are just starting, then put the first month of this calendar year. If you have been in business awhile, then put January of the previous calendar year (if you are a calendar year business). It is helpful to have 12 months of historical financial data to help.

The "Last Closed Month" is the last month of actual financial data such as payroll, bank and credit card transactions, client invoices, and vendor bills.

Step 2: Existing Revenue

When building a forecasting model, it all starts with revenue. I would suggest going back to Chapter 8.

This template uses a more client / service product approach in forecasting. If you sell many different products, you may want to use the product template in Chapter 8.

For purposes of this exercise, I like the client-focused approach as it helps you better think of your clients and recurring business.

1. List your client revenue you have billed since the first month of the model. Use your accounting/billing system to help.

2. Enter all the revenue by client and service/product since the first month of the model.

3. There are reports in the commonly used Accounting Software that help you with this. Look for a report that says Sales or Income by Customer and customize the reports so it provides monthly revenue going back to the first month in the model.

4. After entering the actual revenue, I suggest trending out the revenue through the rest of the current year

or at least 6-12 months. One easy way to do this is to look at the average of the last three months and use this number. Then, make adjustments based on seasonality or any specific contract or customer arrangements that you are aware of.

Step 3: New Business

The next step is essential in understanding the direction of your business.

1. List out all the client prospects who are discussing opportunities. Also, break opportunities by different services or products, if necessary.

2. Determine the annual revenue potential. If you are very unsure, enter an average client annual revenue as a placeholder.

3. Enter the month you think you can close the business. I suggest spreading this out over the following 3-4 months or more. It is not reasonable to assume all new business starts next month.

4. List the probability of closing the business.

   a. 25% is for opportunities that you just started discussing.

   b. 50% is for revenue from services you have pitched where there is significant interest.

   c. 75% if there is a verbal commitment, but the timing may still be unclear.

   d. 90% if you have sent a contract and are awaiting signature.

5. Calculate the revenue based on the number of months of the revenue multiplied by the probability. For example, if you are working on an opportunity that is $36,000 in annual revenue over 12 months and that is 50% probable of close, you will enter $1,500 per month ($36,000 / 12 x 50%).

Step 4: Staffing

For most businesses, staffing expense is the largest expense category. Include all full time and part-time employees as well as contractors in the forecast.

1. List out all names and titles if you have them. Put placeholders for positions you would like to hire.

2. Enter the annual salaries for all employees or annual expected compensation for contractors. Put Employees and Contractors in different sections.

3. Calculate the monthly compensation for each employee.

4. You will notice in this tab, we are starting with the next forecast month. This is because we will know the historical compensation expense when we enter this on the P&L (Profit & Loss) tab.

5. Enter the Hire Date for new employees or contractors so you know when to start including this compensation expense in the model.

Step 5: Profit & Loss (P&L)

1. Enter all revenue and expenses from the actual months that have been reconciled. You may have

to add categories, but keep it simple. At this point, you don't want too many categories, but include the most important ones. You can run a P&L or Income Statement by month in any accounting software. Try downloading it to Excel.

2. Link the existing revenue from this tab to the applicable line on the P&L tab. You will want to do the same for the New Revenue. This will now give you a combined revenue forecast.

3. If you have Cost of Goods Sold, calculate your gross margin amount (Sales – Cost of Goods Sold) and the Gross Margin % (Sales – Cost of Goods Sold) / Sales for each month. Take the average percentage for the last 12 months and use this percentage going forward. You may want to improve your margins or you have to show improvement for the model to work. For now, keep the Gross Margin % the same.

4. For the forecasting months, link the Salary and Contractor tabs to the applicable lines. Put all hourly and part-time employees in the Salary line for now. You can break this out later if it is necessary.

5. **Other Personnel Expenses** – Typically these expenses are based on Salaries.

   a. **Payroll Taxes** – In the US, I use 7.65% of salary expenses. Look at the historical percentage of salary and use this to forecast going forward.

   b. **Fringe Benefits** – This will vary based on if the company pays a percentage of health and dental insurance or provides retirement benefits. Calculate the percentage of fringe benefits / salaries and use this percentage going forward.

c. **Bonus/Commission Expense** – This is dependent on your bonus structure. You can forecast this as a percentage of salaries or revenue depending on how you bonus your employees. Be sure to calculate payroll tax on this.

d. **Recruiting** – If you are hiring quickly and using a recruiter or software, put these expenses here. They can be a significant expense if you are using an Executive Recruiter.

e. **Other Personnel expenses** – Use this for any other employee related expenses not included above. Examples might include employee events.

6. **Other Operating Expenses**

   a. **Advertising / Marketing**
   Web development, social media and online marketing, print, radio, television and any other expenses related to getting the word out about your services and products.

   b. **Travel**
   Vehicle mileage, airfare, hotels, meals during travel, and any other expense related to traveling for business purposes.

   c. **Rent / Building Expenses**
   Any office rent and utilities related to your office or facility. You can also include property taxes and repairs and maintenance.

   d. **Office Supplies**
   Any office related expenses necessary to operate your business. Examples might include paper, keyboards, pens, notebooks, and lower dollar office equipment and furniture. You could put computer

equipment here also. Larger items can be depreciated for both book and tax purposes. We will discuss this later.

e. **Dues & Subscriptions**
Any professional dues paid each year as well as newspaper and magazine subscriptions.

f. **Training**
Any professional development for online or in person conferences or courses. I typically include books in this category.

g. **Telecommunication**
Telephone, mobile phone, and internet related expenses.

h. **Software Costs**
Any software you use to run your business. Many software expenses are subscription based. I would advise putting these expenses here instead of Dues & Subscriptions.

i. **Professional Fees**
Any fees for legal, tax, accounting, marketing, development, or any other consulting.

j. **Business Insurance**
Insurance such as General Liability, Professional Services, Worker's Compensation, Auto, Property, Director's & Officers and any other insurance necessary to run your business.

k. **Miscellaneous Costs**
I am sure I didn't think of everything so this is for many other small expenses. If it becomes a significant category, then start reporting this separate of miscellaneous expenses.

l. **Operating Profit (EBITDA)**
    Revenue less Cost of Goods Sold (COGS) and
    Operating Expenses. You want to review this margin on a regular basis and look to improve it over
    time. It is an important figure for investors to fully
    understand the potential of your business.

m. **Other Income**
    Interest Income or Gain on Sale of any asset.

n. **Interest Expense**
    Interest Expense from a Line of Credit or
    Long-Term loan

o. **Depreciation & Amortization**
    Long term property such as Buildings, Auto,
    Furniture, Vehicles, and Computer Equipment
    that is depreciated over time. Also, this includes
    intangible assets such as software that are amortized over time. Book and Tax rules are different
    here.

p. **Tax Expense**
    Federal and State Tax Expenses

Before going further, most accounting software will allow
you to run your financials based on cash basis which is really
just the income and expense hitting your bank and credit
card. It is easier to understand, but it doesn't give you a great
picture of your business margin on a monthly or quarterly
basis. You may do this for tax purposes.

For operational purposes, I suggest reviewing your financials on accrual basis. If you have to put financials together
based on generally accepted accounting principles (GAAP),
you will want to do this. The biggest reason is that you can
see more clearly your revenue, gross margin, and operating
margin on a monthly basis. It tells you much sooner the

direction of your business and helps with forecasting and planning.

Step 6: Balance Sheet

For some of you, the Balance Sheet might be too much accounting for you. I am not going to get very technical. It is important to look at this report because it tells you so much about where your cash is going. If you simply review the Profit & Loss Statement, you can miss an important part of your financial situation.

1. **Accounts Receivable**

   Most businesses will bill some or all customers and expect payment in 10, 15, 30, or sometimes 60 days. This means that as your business is growing your Accounts Receivable is growing, but it is not translating to cash. Review the change in your Accounts Receivable each month to understand this impact on your cash. Set up a consistent billing and collection process so you are reviewing this regularly.

2. **Prepaid Expenses**

   Sometimes you must pay for something in advance or it is financially beneficial to do so. Examples might be conferences, travel, insurance, software, and dues / subscriptions. Typically, you get a price break by paying in advance, so you want to plan to have the cash to take advantage of this. If your prepaid expenses are increasing, it will affect your cash.

3. **Inventory**

   If you have a services business, then skip this one. If you buy any materials and products that are then sold to customers either directly or as part of manufactured or assembled products, then you need to measure your inventory. This will help you calculate your Cost of Goods Sold. As inventory increases, it will lower your cash. On the other hand, if your inventory is decreasing, you might have more cash but need to be prepared to buy more inventory which makes forecasting essential.

4. **Property & Equipment**
   As your business grows, you might decide to purchase a building, land, furniture, vehicles, equipment, computers, etc. All of this affects your cash flow. It should be depreciated for both operational and tax purposes. Forecasting these types of purchases will have a significant effect on cash flow.

5. **Accumulated Deprecation**
   This is a negative number than is the sum of your depreciation over time. The purpose is to calculate your net book value of the Property and Equipment. You can calculate this by category and it will carry over from previous years. This is necessary when doing a GAAP financial statement. Please note that GAAP depreciation may be expensed evenly over the life of the asset but tax depreciation is typically under an accelerated depreciation method. This means that GAAP depreciation is different than tax depreciation in most cases. A good bookkeeper can help you get his set up if you need more help.

6. **Accounts Payable**
   Just as you might extend credit with your customers; your suppliers, vendors, or partners will do the same for you. You can manage cash flow well if your Accounts Payable terms are longer than Accounts Receivable. If your Accounts Payable is growing, you may deceivingly have more cash in your bank. Of course, the bills

will have to get paid so understanding your Accounts Payable trends are helpful.

7. **Accrued Liabilities**

This is a broad category for any liability you might have to pay in the future. This could be payroll related, such as bonuses or commissions or payroll taxes. It might be for professional fees such as accounting, legal or consulting. Even accruing federal, state, property, or sales tax is helpful for managing future cash flow outlays.

8. **Short & Long-Term Debt**
Short-Term debt is anything you borrow that needs to be paid back in less than a year. A perfect example is a bank line of credit.

Long-Term debt is anything you borrowed that is due over time for more than a year. This might be financing for vehicles, equipment, building, or business loans.

9. **Invested Capital**
When you start a business, typically investors and owners need to start with seed money. This is invested capital. If you need to put more money into the business to keep it running, you would account for it here.

10. **Distributions**
As a business owner or investor, we look forward to distributions. This means the business is truly profitable with good margins. Any kind of disbursement to owners or dividends are put here. Sometimes personal expenses are processed through a business account. You would account for these expenses here in many cases. I would recommend processing any personal expenses out of another bank account or credit card that is separate from your business.

Distributions is a good place to look if your business is profitable, but there is no cash in the bank account. We should take distributions regularly but be sure to have a controlled process around it. The best method is to get to a point where you pay yourself a distribution quarterly based on profits. Then, it is easier to control and forecast cash flow.

11. **Retained Earnings**
This is a calculated number of all your Net Income since you started your business. It is calculated by taking the previous month Retained Earnings balance and adding the current month Net Income.

Step 7: Cash Flows

The Statement of Cash Flows can be even more confusing to those with little or no accounting knowledge. The most important thing to know is the purpose of the three main categories. This report will tell you where your cash is going from operating activities, investing activities, and financing activities.

1. **Operating Activities**
Operating activities are the sum of your profit (Net Income) and changes in the current assets and liabilities. Current assets include Accounts Receivable, Inventory, Accounts Payables, Prepaid Expenses and Accrued Expenses.

This is an important metric because it can quickly tell you why you might be low on cash. You could be very profitable, but have a decrease in cash from operating activities. The report will show you how your cash could be increasing due to slower Accounts

Receivable collections or increases in Inventory. With this information, you can develop a plan and system to manage cash in these areas.

2. **Investing Activities**
   Many businesses eventually need to purchase equipment, furniture, computer, vehicles, and even buildings and land. This category will also include any debt financing and principle payments.

   You could be a highly profitable business and even manage your operating cash well, but still be siphoning cash out of your business. If you purchase fixed assets, this may not be bad if this is necessary. If you are having to make large principle payments, this could be a larger debt issue. Too much debt in your business definitely will affect your ability to reinvest in the growth of your business.

3. **Financing Activities**
   Finally, financial activities are any cash added to your business from investors, partners, or the owner. It also includes any distributions and dividends.

   It is entirely possible, especially in a small single owner business, that the business is profitable, operating well with little debt or capital purchases, but is still losing cash.

   This most commonly happens through owner distributions. Sometimes, the owner may use the business card or bank account for personal purchases which is effectively a distribution. As mentioned above, it is best to avoid comingling business and personal expenses and take distributions in a more consistent and organized way based on profits.

The Ever-Changing Financial Model

Almost as fast as the weather, your financial forecast will change. You will build the model and get a new customer, employee, or have a new project. This financial model is meant to be easily updated as the business changes. You will want to enter actual financials as these trends will also affect your business.

I strongly encourage anyone to build a tool such as this for your decision making. Don't over-complicate it so you never do it or you only do it once and never look at it again. The basics mentioned in this section will save you time, provide you peace, give you clarity, and position your business toward growth and success. Who doesn't want that?

If you find that you are getting stuck on any of these steps above try the following:

1. Check out our "Forecast Your Future Course" at **www.forecastyourfuturecourse.com** to get video, worksheets, and a community of support to guide and direct you.

2. Find a fractional or part-time CFO that can help you put this together. Some CPAs can help in this area, but make sure it is someone that has some operational experience and is not only focused on tax preparation.

3. Technology has made it possible and quite effective to provide CFO services anywhere in the world. Through screen sharing, video conferencing, and cloud-based networking, you don't have to visit face to face. I have found some of my most effective meetings to be through remote screen share. Contact me at **www.bendercfoservices.com** and we can discuss further a more tailored CFO Services approach.

APPENDIX 2

CALL TO CLARITY QUESTIONS

Part 1: Understand Where You Are Today

Ch. 1: Lessons from a Squirrel and a Drain Clog

Take some time now to write down at least five reasons you started and want to grow your business. Keep this in a place you can visit regularly.

Ch. 2: Financial Mindset Matters

Write down at least one limiting belief you have financially, and then write an empowering thought to replace it.

Ch. 3: Overcome Fear of the Numbers

Think of one thing you fear regarding your business finances. How can you embrace this fear and be courageous?

Ch. 4: 10 Ways Businesses Act Like a Teenager

Of the 10 ways mentioned in this chapter, which one resonates with you? How might you keep yourself from falling into this trap?

Ch. 5: Developing an Abundance Mindset Through Life's Changes

Do you embrace change easily? Which of the five reasons change is good is the most motivating and why?

Ch. 6: Common Small Business Financial Questions

What is one financial issue you want to solve in your business?

Part 2: Determine Your Destination

Ch. 7: To Plan or Not to Plan

Do you plan too much or too little? What adjustments are needed so that you can begin measuring your business results against expectations?

Ch. 8: It All Starts with Revenue

Have you built a prospecting plan? If so, review and update it and schedule time to do this on a regular basis. If not, get started today because this may be the most important exercise that can build clarity in your business.

Ch. 9: How to Spend Wisely

Do you know your current monthly recurring expenses? If not, I suggest finding a bookkeeper to help you get organized.

Ch. 10: Ways to Focus on Profits

Review your expenses and find an area where you should look to save. Most likely one of the above categories is worth taking a second look.

Ch. 11: Where is the Cash Going?

Do you struggle with cash flow? What is the top area of concern from those mentioned in this chapter? If still uncertain, review your Balance Sheet or contact a good financial consultant or fractional CFO who can help.

Part 3: How Do You Reach Your Destination Faster?

Ch. 12: How to Stay Disciplined and Focused

Take one of the discipline habits as mentioned in this chapter and put it on the schedule. Practice this discipline regularly and eventually it will become a new, good habit.

Ch. 13: Focus on Strengths

Take the Strengths Finder 2.0 assessment to know your strengths. If you have already done this, review it and write down one area where you can maximize one of your strengths.

Ch. 14: Why Consistency is Powerful

What is one consistent business activity that you want to start to implement? It could be a consistent accounting, marketing, business development activity or maybe something more related to personal health.

Ch. 15: What Can We Do to Add Value

Pick one thing that you want to start doing that will help you add value to your clients, customers, employees, etc.

Ch. 16: The Keys to Productive Improvements

Pick one productivity improvement to focus on developing. Is it to get rid of debt, improve automation, or to utilize delegation?

Ch. 17: How Focused Goals Help You Move Faster

What is something that you do that sabotages your goals? Recognize it and choose one method to help you stay on track.

Part 4: Assess and Adjust

Ch. 18: Keeping Score

Pick at least one key performance indicator that you want to start reviewing regularly. Make sure it is something that you easily track and will be motivating and helpful in your business.

Ch. 19: Business Development Plan

Block out time each week for business development. Try something new or come up with a weekly plan that you can implement that will keep new opportunities coming to your business.

Ch. 20: Goals Assessment

Take time to assess and adjust any goal that is not working. If you don't have any revenue or profit goal for your business, set one and develop a plan to reach this goal.

Ch. 21: The Financial Model

If you do not have a forecast model for your business, get started as soon as possible. Look at Appendix 1 for more help or hire a professional. Make it easy to update with actual changes in your business.

Ch. 22: A Useful Dashboard

Take the KPI that you decided was important in Chapter 18 and develop a quick dashboard. It might be a chart or a graph. Connect your dashboard to your financial model so it changes as your model changes. Once again, don't over-complicate it. A dashboard is best designed to be easy to read and understand.

Ch. 23: Ideas to Stay on Track

Pick one good habit to implement and keep track of how you are doing. Habits take longer than you think to form so try doing it consistently over the next three months.

Ch. 24: Next Steps to Growth

Pick one thing that you are going to do in the next day to help you positively impact the future in your business.

NOTES

Ch. 2: Financial Mindset Matters

Port, Michael. 2015. *Steal The Show: How to Guarantee A Standing Ovation For All The Performances In Your Life.* New York: Houghton Mifflin Harcourt.

Ch. 3: Overcome Fear of the Numbers

Smith, Paul. 2012. *Lead with a Story: A Guide to Crafting Business Narratives That Captivate, Convince and Inspire.* New York: American Managment Association.

Ch. 4: 10 Ways Business Act Like a Teenager

Mind Tools Content Team. 2018. *How to Make Decisions.* March 14. https://www.mindtools.com/pages/article/newTED_00.htm.

Riel, Jennifer & Roger L. Martin. 2017. *Creating Great Choices: A Leader's Guide to Integrative Thinking.* Boston: Harvard Business Review Press.

Ch. 5: Developing an Abundance Mindset Through Life's Changes

Covey, Stephen R. 2017. *The 7 Habits of Highly Effective People: Powerful Lessons in Personal Change (Infographics Edition)*. FranklinCovey Co.

Hyatt, Michael & Daniel Harkavy. 2016. *Living Forward*. Grand Rapids: Baker Books.

Ch. 7: To Plan or Not to Plan

Sivers, Derek. 2011. *Anything You Want: 40 Lessons for a New Kind of Entrepreneur*. New York: Portfolio/ Penguin.

Ch. 9: How to Spend Wisely

Michalowicz, Mike. 2014,2017. *"Profit First: Transform Your Business From a Cash Eating Monster to a Money-Making Machine"*. New York: Portfolio Penguin.

UBS Investor Watch. 2015. "UBS." *When is enough… enough? Why the wealthy can't get off the tread-mill.* 2Q. https://www.ubs.com/content/dam/ WealthManagementAmericas/documents/ investor-watch-2Q2015.pdf.

Ch. 10: Ways to Focus on Profits

Michalowicz, Mike. 2014,2017. *"Profit First: Transform Your Business From a Cash Eating Monster to a Money-Making Machine."* New York: Portfolio Penguin.

Ch. 11: Where is the Cash Going?

Michalowicz, Mike. 2014,2017. *"Profit First: Transform Your Business From a Cash Eating Monster to a Money-Making Machine."* New York: Portfolio Penguin.

Ramsey, Dave. 2013. *The Total Money Makeover: A Proven Plan for Financial Fitness.* Nelson Books.

Ch. 12: How to Stay Disciplined and Focused

Cardone, Grant. 2011. *10X Rule: The Only Difference Between Success and Failure.* John Wiley & Sons.

Dumas, John Lee. 2017. *The Mastery Journal: Master Productivity, Discipline, and Focus in 100 Days.* John Lee Dumas.

Hyatt, Michael. 2016. "Free to Focus Online Course." *Free to Focus: Achieve More By Doing Less.* Michael Hyatt & Co.

Hyatt, Michael & Daniel Harkavy. 2016. *Living Forward.* Grand Rapids: Baker Books.

Ch. 13: Focus on Strengths

Covey, Stephen R. 2017. *The 7 Habits of Highly Effective People: Powerful Lessons in Personal Change (Infographics Edition).* FranklinCovey Co.

Rath, Tom. 2007. *StrengthsFinder 2.0.* New York: Gallup Press.

Ch. 14: Why Consistency is Powerful

Bayles, David & Ted Orland. 1993. *Art & Fear: Observations on the Perils (and Rewards) of Artmaking.*

Olson, Jeff. 2005-2013. *The Slight Edge: Turning Simple Disciplines Into Massive Success & Happiness.* Austin, TX: Greenleaf Book Group Press.

Stanley, Thomas J. and William D. Danko. 1996. *The Millionaire Next Door.* Pocket Books, a division of Simon & Schuster.

Ch. 15: What Can We Do to Add Value?

Ally, Daniel. 2016. *5 Tips to Read 100 Books a Year.* April 4. https://www.success.com/blog/5-tips-to-read-100-books-a-year.

Beaudine, Bob. 2016. *2 Chairs: The Secret That Changes Everything.* Worthy Publishing Group, a division of Worthy Media, Inc.

Elrod, Hal. 2017. *The Miracle Morning: The Not-So-Obvious Secret Guaranteed to Transform Your Life Before 8am.* Hal Elrod International.

Olson, Jeff. 2005-2013. *The Slight Edge: Turning Simple Disciplines Into Massive Success & Happiness.* Austin, TX: Greenleaf Book Group Press.

Ch. 16: The Keys to Productive Improvements

Gerber, Michael. 1995. *The E-Myth Revisited: Why Most Small Business Don't Work and What to Do About It.* New York: HarperCollins.

Hooser, Phllip Van. 2018. *Leaders Ought to Know.* March 26. http://www.leadersoughttoknow.com/tag/levels-of-empowerment/.

Lencioni, Patrick. 2012. *The Advantage: Why Organizational Health Trumps Everything Else in Business.* San Francisco: Jossey-Bass.

Maxwell, John. 1998 and 2017. *The 21 Irrefutable Laws of Leadership.* Nashville: Thomas Nelson.

Statistic Brain. 2017. May 5. https://www.statisticbrain.com/startup-failure-by-industry/.

Ch. 17: How Focused Goals Help You Move Faster

Covey, Stephen R., A. Roger Merrill, and Rebecca R. Merrill. 1994. *First Thing First.* London: Simon & Schuster.

Dumas, John Lee. 2015. *The Freedom Journal: Accomplish Your #1 Goal in 100 Days.* John Lee Dumas.

Hyatt, Michael. 2015. *5 Days to Your Best Year Ever.* https://bestyearever.me/.

Hyatt, Michael. 2018. *Full Focus Planner.* Michael Hyatt & Company.

Hyatt, Michael. 2018. *Your Best Year Ever: A 5-Step Plan for Achieving Your Most Important Goals.* Baker Books.

Port, Michael. 2015. *Steal The Show: How to Guarantee A Standing Ovation For All The Performances In Your Life.* New York: Houghton Mifflin Harcourt.

White, Ray. 2014. *Connecting Happiness and Success: A Guide to Creating Success Through Happiness.* Xilo Media.

Ch. 18: Keeping Score

Dumas, John Lee & Jordan Harbinger. Accessed: March 27, 2018. *Podcast 1190: Freedom is an art, and Jordan Harbinget is da Vinci.* https://www.eofire.com/podcast/jordanharbingerfreedom/.

Marr, Bernard. 2013. *The 75 KPIs Every Manager Needs to Know.* September 5. https://www.linkedin.com/pulse/20130905053105-64875646-the-75-kpis-every-manager-needs-to-know/

Ch. 19: Business Development Plan

Brunson, Russell. 2015. *Dotcom Secrets: The Underground Playbook for Growing Your Company Online.* New York: Morgan James.

Cardone, Grant. 2011. *10X Rule: The Only Difference Between Success and Failure.* John Wiley & Sons.

Covey, Stephen R. 2017. *The 7 Habits of Highly Effective People: Powerful Lessons in Personal Change (Infographics Edition).* FranklinCovey Co.

Intuit. 2016. *Intuit Research Reveals Five Trends Shaping the Future of Small Business.* October 20. https://www.businesswire.com/news/home/20161020005548/en/Golden-Age-Small-Business.

McKay, Brett & Kate. 2013. *The Eisenhower Decision Matrix: How to Distingush Between Urgent and Important Tasks and Make Real Progress in Your Life.* October 23. https://www.artofmanliness.com/2013/10/23/eisenhower-decision-matrix/.

Pofeldt, Elaine. 2016. *Why Small Business Ownership will Skyrocket in 10 years Especially by Solopreneurs.* October 24. https://www.forbes.com/sites/elainepofeldt/2016/10/24/why-small-business-ownership-will-skyrocke t-in-10-years-especially-by-solopreneurs/#6dcce9716dba.

Schrader, Brendon. 2015. *Here's Why The Freelancer Economy Is On The Rise.* August 15. https://www.fastcompany.com/3049532/heres-why-the-freelancer-economy-i s-on-the-rise.

Ch. 20: Goals Assessment

Hyatt, M. 2018. *Your Best Year Ever: A 5-Step Plan for Achieving Your Most Important Goals.* Baker Books..

Hyatt, Michael & Daniel Harkavy. 2016. *Living Forward.* Grand Rapids: Baker Books.

Ch. 21: The Financial Model

Riel, Jennifer & Roger L. Martin. 2017. *Creating Great Choices: A Leader's Guide to Integrative Thinking.* Boston: Harvard Business Review Press.

Ch. 23: Ideas to Stay on Track

Access March 30, 2018. *Best-selling book of non-fiction.* http://www.guinnessworldrecords.com/world-records/best-selling-book-of-non-fiction/.

Duhigg, Charles. 2012. *The Power of Habit: Why We Do What We Do In Life And Business.* New York: Random House.

Dumas, John Lee. 2015. *The Freedom Journal: Master Accomplish Your Goal in 100 Days.* John Lee Dumas.

Hyatt, Michael & Daniel Harkavy. 2016. *Living Forward.* Grand Rapids: Baker Books.

Ziglar Inc. Access March 30, 2018. *484: Joshua Spodek - The massive power of habitually doing what you don't have to do.* https://ziglarshow.com/?s=Joshua+Spodek.

Ch. 24: Next Steps to Growth

Mercola, Dr. 2015. *5 Reasons to Spend More Time Outside - Even When It's Cold.* March 6. https://fitness.mercola.com/sites/fitness/archive/2015/03/06/spending-time-outdoors.aspx.

Smith, Paul. 2012. *Lead with a Story: A Guide to Crafting Business Narratives That Captivate, Convince and Inspire.* New York: American Managment Association.

FORECAST YOUR FUTURE COURSE

Do you want a more hands on approach to help your business be more financially successful?

Do you learn better through videos, activities, and a community of support?

Does the forecasting model seem overwhelming and you want a slower, bite-sized approach to building your business for financial success?

If any of the above questions is a "Yes", we have built a course that has the following:

- Videos broken out by module and lesson

- Each lesson is designed to take less than 30 minutes

- Downloadable worksheet

- Downloadable forecasting templates

- Online community of business owners and support

- Other bonuses and coaching opportunities based on needs and interests

I encourage you to sign up for the Forecast Your Future Course. Go to the following site to learn more:

www.forecastyourfuturecourse.com

Bender CFO Services Inc.

Bender CFO Services provides finance and accounting services for small businesses such as:

- Financial Forecasting & Modeling
- Financial Reporting & Analysis
- Expense Review and Management
- Accounting Staff Training and Supervision
- Strategic Planning and Consulting
- Financial Process Improvement and Controls

Our services allow you to focus on running your business without the need to hire full-time accounting staff such as Accountants, Controllers, or even a CFO.

Bender CFO Services is not a CPA Firm.

Connect at the following places:

Email: **shane@bendercfoservices.com**
LinkedIn: **linkedin.com/in/shanefbender**
Website: **bendercfoservices.com**
FaceBook: **facebook.com/bendercfo/**
Twitter: @ShaneFBender